Essex*Works*.
For a better quality of life
WKF

Please return this book on or before the date shown above. To
renew go to www.essex.gov.uk/libraries, ring 0845 603 7628 or
go to any Essex library.

Essex County Council

Days Like This

A Memoir

Nicholas Owen

Blenheim Press Limited
Codicote

Published in 2012
by
Blenheim Press Ltd
Codicote Innovation Centre
St Albans Road
Codicote
Herts SG4 8WH
www.blenheimpressltd.co.uk

ISBN 978-1-906302-23-8

Typeset by TW Typesetting, Plymouth, Devon

Cover pictures by Andy Newbold Photography, Leatherhead

Printed and bound by CPI Group (UK) Ltd, Croydon, CR0 4YY

Dedication

For Brenda, Rebecca, Justine, Daniel, Anthony –
and my grandchildren.

INTRODUCTION

Passing my 65th birthday seems a good moment to try to make sense of the days of my life. It leads inevitably to apologies. I am all too aware that many who have played important parts are not actually named in this book. I hope all will forgive, and know that they join those mentioned in having my gratitude for making the many days so wonderfully interesting.

I have worked for a succession of extraordinarily indulgent bosses, in a trade that is usually thought so hard-nosed and flint-hearted. I am very grateful to them, as well as to the friends and relatives who have ensured that, in the main, the rest of life has been very good.

My thanks too for the help and advice of Alan McMullen at Blenheim Press and my photographer pal Andy Newbold.

All reporters must acknowledge occasional mistakes in their work. I am sure there will be some errors and omissions in this memoir. They are entirely my responsibility.

Finally, my wife has encouraged me constantly to press on with this project, and has put up with the hours of effort that have gone into its completion. My love, I thank you.

Nicholas Owen
Reigate, 2012

ONE

My Uncle Eric always had trouble with bonfires. One drowsy afternoon he was struggling as usual with a huge pile of stuff that should have roared away. He was down at the end of his long and unkempt garden. Bonfires should be the most glorious fun for small boys. There was to be no fun that day. I was told not to go wandering off to help. My Auntie Joan had something important to say to me.

As we sat near the back of her house, Joan smiled, and reminded me that my mother had been very unwell for a long time. I did not need to be told. I had started to get extremely anxious about her. My aunt must have agonised over the words to use next. 'Nicky,' she said. 'Mummy's gone to heaven.'

Next memory: we were back inside the house. I was sitting in one chair, kicking at a fly crawling around on the back of another. I was crying so much my insides hurt. I remember little else. I don't remember, for instance, when my father appeared. Or whether I was taken to him. Or what he said to me. And in those days no-one dreamed of taking a small child to a parent's funeral. Auntie Joan herself was to die of cancer not many years later.

There has been so much laughter in my life. Yet over and over again in that summer and autumn of 1955 when I was eight years old the tears poured: for my dead mother, for my own shock, and for my loneliness when I was abruptly sent away to a boarding school. I have always struggled to understand the decisions my father took in the days and weeks after he lost his young wife. And I have struggled to try to etch in the details of the elusive person who had been my mother.

My few recollections are of a woman with large round glasses who coughed a good deal. Digging through the family photograph albums I find a host of black and white pictures of her. A pretty teenager with her parents and sisters, often wearing a pair of the wiry spectacles that were so common then. There she is marrying my father when he was home

1

from war service briefly in 1943. Her with me on holidays, sometimes with the wind tearing at the mane of her dark hair. My favourite picture is a professional one. I guess the studio photographer had suggested she look at something in the corner of the room. She appears as if gazing into an unknowable future. Her eyes are bright. She looks happy.

Mum had two sisters and a brother. Uncle Ron was always another distant figure from the innumerable black and white snaps. He died just before I was born, killed by tuberculosis, which carried off so many in those days. My mother got progressively more sick, and even a small child could sense that her health was fragile. I have a hideously clear memory of looking up at her during a walk in the avenue near our home. She had, as so often, stopped and begun coughing, hard. 'You won't die, will you Mummy?' She smiled at me. 'Of course not.' You should not make promises you cannot keep. It is something I have said a million times. Yet we all do it, especially when talking to children. Mum had suffered rheumatic fever in the 1930s. Family talk was that she had been warned against giving birth. I was her only child, and my arrival could hardly have made her stronger. She insisted on having me. My thought has always been that I hastened her end.

The tears that literally choke can come often in childhood. If you are lucky, they are rare when you are an adult. For me, they did come many, many years later when, during my own brush with a frightening disease, I found myself crying helplessly. Not for myself, but curiously enough for my father, bereaved young, and dead himself nearly thirty years before.

The way life turned upside down in the 1950s was a foretaste of how it would always lurch around. I grew up in and around a London very different from today. For sixty years and more, I have taken a series of sharp turns, and swayed and wobbled through contrasting experiences. There was certainly too much death and illness, too early. Schools were strikingly different, pleasant and grim. And yet I have also been wonderfully lucky. I only ever wanted to be a journalist. To have been one for almost half a century, in newspapers and on television, has been a marvellous experience. For all the pain, there has been so much to enjoy, to laugh about. And to make others laugh too, now and then. Even the Queen herself. How it all came about is to reflect on a rollercoaster of a life.

TWO

My father's names were a curiosity. He was Wallace Thomas Owen, or W. T. Owen, on all correspondence and other documents. Yet no-one ever called him Wallace. 'Tom' always. Yet when Dad died, I discovered that on his birth certificate he had been Thomas Wallace all along. Just one puzzle. There would be more.

My Dad had been a Navy man. After schooldays he had joined the RNVR, the Royal Naval Volunteer Reserve. When the Second World War broke out he was 19 and went straight into the regular Royal Navy. He seemed to have been involved in just about every action that counted: Atlantic convoys, Arctic convoys, the surrender of the Italian fleet, the

Dad, in his wartime naval uniform . . . note the cigarette!

Normandy landings. In 1944 he was in a curious hybrid unit that brought Navy and Army together. He was bucketing along in a Jeep through recently-liberated Holland when it hit a mine. Lieutenant Tom Owen had already been torpedoed twice. This time, he was badly injured. To the end of his days there were thin blue scars across his forehead. His hearing was affected by the explosion. There was another long-lasting legacy of his Navy days. Some emergency dental work had to be done in a hurry in Ireland earlier in the war. The dentist was a lousy hygienist. My father was left with gum disease that he had to endure for the next 40 years.

In 1945, Dad was in Australia, headed for the conflict still going on with the Japanese when Hiroshima and Nagasaki were attacked with nuclear weapons. Tom Owen was free to return home. Goodness knows if he would have survived had Japan gone on and on sacrificing untold numbers of their own people as well as their enemies. I say, God bless President Truman who authorised the atom bomb missions that ended the war.

Dad had married Edna Frisby during his short leave in 1943, and I appeared on February 10th, 1947. In the depths of Britain's coldest winter of the 20th century I was born in Islington, North London, in a

My mother, around the time she married father in 1943.

hospital much later transformed into swanky housing. The location makes me a Cockney. A taxi driver once berated me for speaking so plummy and posh on the TV, so unlike the nice ordinary voice of a genuine Londoner like himself. 'So where were you born?' I asked him. 'Silvertown, mate.' Way out in Dockland, when it had real docks in it, mind. I took great pleasure in telling an astonished cabbie I was as much a Cockney as he was.

But then he had never met Grandma Owen, Dad's mother. A real Londoner, born Elsie North, she came from the West End, though not one of the sprauncy bits. A recent discovery was that her family were in the funeral trade. My beloved grandmother, a tiny woman so unlike her four children, remained sharp and active almost to the day she died, aged just short of 101. She would have been furious if I had dropped an 'h', or missed the 'g' of any word ending in 'ing'. Or if I'd called a phone a 'dog' (dog and bone, if you are not aware), or a suit a 'whistle' (whistle and flute), or described my wife as 'the trouble and strife.' Grandma Owen was an unyielding believer not just in the ways you should speak, but also how you should behave and dress. My Dad inherited her values and they were dinned into me. Any hat or cap was to be doffed when a lady was present. Doors had to be opened for women, seats offered. Stand up when a woman comes to your restaurant table. Grandma was particularly fanatical about shoes. Always have them well polished, she would say. You can get away with a lot if you have clean shoes.

Her grandparents were servants at Corsham Court in Wiltshire, a rambling stately home you can pay a few pounds to visit today. My great great paternal grandfather, head groom to Lord Methuen back in the mid 19th century, was a Mr Arundel, which explains where I get my third Christian name after Nicholas and David. David could be a nod towards Welsh ancestors; Nicholas possibly associated with the French ancestors of my mother's family. Long-living is the striking feature of the women in Grandma Owen's line. My Grandma's 100 followed her mother who survived to her century, and before her Mrs Arundel, at Corsham Court, who managed 104.

Grandma's husband Robert Owen came from a family who had been in the dairy business, as were so many Welsh folk who emigrated to London in Victorian times. Robert was a chauffeur to two grand ladies for many years. He was in almost at the dawn of motoring and, though a fiercely moral man, he loved to tell tales of misdeeds and misfortunes from the early 1900s.

With Grandma Owen, on her 100th birthday.

Grandad Owen, chauffeur.

First there was the notice he kept of a fine of £5 he had received for speeding, doing twelve rather than ten miles an hour. He explained how three policemen would hide in hedges a few hundred yards apart. As you passed the first one, he would step out behind you and wave a flag for the second copper to start a stopwatch running. If the car covered the distance between PC One and PC Two too quickly, the second bobby would wave another flag. PC Three would hop out and stop you. Five pounds was a heck of a lot of money for young Robert Owen, more than a week's wages. His employers paid the fine. All very different from the policing that my own son would do after he joined the Metropolitan force a hundred or so years later. Except I can't help noticing that rather a lot of police officers still seem to spend their time at the roadsides, using speed cameras to catch out motorists, a modern variation on the theme of shooting ducks in a proverbial barrel.

Robert's tussles with the law did not end with that fine. Because of the tough limits, early cars were fitted with speed governors. The trick, Grandad explained to me, was to wait until you left built-up areas, so infested with policemen. Then you would stop, go under the bonnet and remove the bolts that screwed down a governor designed to keep the throttle from being opened up too far. Off you could go at perhaps 20 miles an hour, as long as the tyres, the cylinder block, the radiator and goodness knows what else held out. Garages were almost non-existent so you had to carry your own spares and tools, and know how to use them.

On another eventful day in south London Grandad collided with a bridegroom. It had been raining hard. The uneven road surface was glassily wet. The bridegroom for some reason left the church to cross the road, right in front of Robert and his car. Vehicles then only had brakes on one of the four wheels. Hitting the brake pedal swept the car into an immediate spin. The groom was skittled over, though the only damage was to his wedding day dignity.

My father was the youngest of three brothers. If to most people he was Tom, his mother and father and most relatives called him 'Bay', short for 'baby.' In the 1930s he and his brothers left their elementary school at 14. A short education by modern standards. Yet they had been taught to love books, plays, and poetry. My father's oldest brother Eric was the most artistic, eventually earning his living as a commercial artist. The next brother was named Robert (always Bob) after his father. He became an author and publisher. He married Dinah, already known to the Owens because she was one of his cousins. They had two daughters, and their love of horses prompted my Uncle Bob to start a series of books explaining riding to youngsters and their bill-paying parents. Bob branched out from writing and publishing horse books into judging at shows – he was a great pinner-on of rosettes – and in retirement, he gave advice about it all on local radio. The strange part was he never sat on a horse.

The Owens ended up in Anerley, close to Crystal Palace in south London. It was there that amateur dramatics brought my mother and my father together. He and brother Bob were the kingpins of a drama group that tended to tackle Shakespeare rather than much light stuff. There are pictures of Dad as a tubby Malvolio. Brother Bob had the matinee idol looks. And knew it. One old photo shows a jaunty grin under a rakish moustache. The hair is jet black, crinkly, and beautifully combed. My uncle was leaning casually on a 1930s suburban mantlepiece as if he was in some mansion in the Hollywood Hills.

Living not far away was the Frisby family. Edna Frisby joined the drama group and fell in love with Dad in the process. How I would love to have a picture of her then. I have searched in vain for her face among the players as they tackled the classics. If my father was, in those days at least, the extrovert, she was not. He was out on stage. She was behind the scenes, a tantalising ghost: somewhere close yet invisible among the young and enthusiastic faces on those makeshift stages more than 70 years ago. Amateur performing got into the blood. I was an enthusiastic amateur actor for several years. Occasionally I would be asked to take my turn painting sets, hunting down props, flogging tickets. I know I should have done. The limelight was what I enjoyed. And so it was for Dad and even more so for the debonair Bob.

Edna's family were more obvious Cockneys. Grandad Frisby's people worked as porters in the Billingsgate and Borough markets. Billingsgate, where so much fish was traded it made the streets all around the north end of London Bridge slippery, decamped years ago to Docklands. Borough Market lives on. At weekends in recent years trendy Londoners have paid amazing prices for fancy food that you used to find only in French street markets. Family stories relate how Grandad Frisby's father was born in a covered wagon in the Borough Market. He was most likely a gipsy. My grandfather was a spare little fellow. He was famous for his dancing, performing with an amateur troupe of soft-shoe shufflers. He

Dancing feet: Grandad Frisby.

could still do the steps in his 90s. At that age he could also nip up and down the spiral stairs in our house, which could be so troublesome to much younger folk. I would come to love the stage. I have always felt I had some of Tom Frisby's extrovert genes.

Whether or not he dreamed of a lifetime in entertainment, in 1914 he went to war. He was keen on horses, and managed to get an appropriate job. The British army didn't send mounted soldiers into battle. He joined the Royal Artillery and rode out among the troops who pulled the big guns into position so they could lay down the barrages that preceded the infantry advances. The casualty rates for those going 'over the top' were frightful. Not being sent into the trenches, Tom survived a war that left him with a great love of horses. Not that he ever owned, or regularly rode one after that war. Which made him very similar to horse expert Uncle Bob.

Tom Frisby made his living first as an optical equipment salesman, later as an employee of a national newspaper. Which meant he was to have the most direct influence on what I did with my working life. And it was with him that another great influence was born. I held tightly to Grandad's hand as we stood on Kent House station and watched the

Golden Arrow express pound through, at its front a gleaming steam engine. The memory is as clear now as the experience some sixty years ago, helping to kindle a passion for railways that has lasted ever since.

My two grandfathers were quite different. Tom Frisby was friendly and outgoing. Robert Owen was much quieter. Being a driver meant he wasn't called up during the First World War. Instead he drove lorries, and afterwards returned to the chauffeuring, which lasted until he retired. He had done so by the time I came along. I only remember being driven by him once. My father was not around one day, so Robert took charge of our unreliable Morris Ten on some careful jaunt through the London suburbs. That car frightened the life out of me once. As we climbed the steep Titsey Hill down in Surrey one afternoon, with me and my Grandmother Owen in the back, the differential exploded, right beneath my feet. There was a bang and a cloud of dust. Suddenly we were not edging upwards but rolling backwards. Dad steered us to a stop against the bank. Ever after we went miles out of our way to avoid the worst of the hills that abounded in our part of the world.

THREE

After my birth, my parents and I lived first with Nana and Grandad Frisby in Reddons Road, Beckenham. The street wasn't made up in those days, and wouldn't be for most of my childhood. You would navigate large potholes in the roadway and along the pavements to reach their comfortable semi of the sort that working class people could then afford. Times and places change. It is now an expensive and smart suburb where house prices in the 1990s didn't so much rise as explode.

After Reddons Road came a flat above a shop in a parade at North Cheam – I can take you to it today, even though I was in a pram myself when we lived there – before mother and father got their first house in

Mother and I, probably on the Kent coast about 1950.

Selsdon, Surrey. Another very early memory was lying in my bed in Selsdon with Dad leaning over to kiss me goodnight, dressed in his RNVR uniform. I was terrified. Was there another war starting? Much later I was to realise he was heading for a long and jolly reunion dinner with old mates from the Navy. A child sees only terrors.

In a way that must be hard to grasp for anyone under about the age of 60, Britain's wartime experience dominated just about everything people said and did, and even the way many places looked. One day, my father showed me a large area of the City still in ruins from German bombing. Today, it is where the Barbican development stands. Every adult talked in terms of 'before the war', 'during the war', and so on.

I was thrilled by the many magazines that were in everyone's houses, recounting wartime exploits. There were loads of black and white pictures, usually of grinning British servicemen and women in some exotic foreign spot. Once I could read, I could thread together the events from the outbreak of war, through the Battle of Britain and the Blitz to Montgomery's victory at El Alamein, the Allied invasion of Normandy, and the eventual Nazi surrender. Recent and most dramatic history was vivid indeed.

So many homes had been bombed or badly damaged that many people found getting somewhere to live was very difficult. In our very small house in Selsdon, we had a lodger, as so many householders did. Who he was, where he worked, how old he was, I now have no idea. All I knew was that he showed me how he could blow perfect smoke rings. Almost every grown-up smoked. Throughout the 1950s and into the 1960s it was an established ritual that when visiting aunts, uncles, and grandparents, as soon as everyone sat down, cigarettes would be offered round as a matter of course: 'Have one of mine . . .' 'No, no, I've already opened this pack . . .'

I saw very little strong drink taken. I think my Owen grandparents disapproved of alcohol. It was a family joke that at Christmas Grandad would leave his accustomed place by the fire – where he would sit hour after hour puffing at his pipe, which was always in need of re-lighting – to go to a sideboard and pour out some ginger wine. It was an indulgence that seemed quite frivolous. Grandad had a reputation for being a stern master in his own house, who would have been astonished if anyone had suggested he rise from his fireside chair to help prepare a meal, or do any washing-up. Stern as he was, he would very often tuck a half crown (12 ½ pence) into my hand as I was about to be taken home.

The country had of course been devastated economically by the Second World War. Rationing was a tedious result. I would watch my mother as she sorted out her ration book before we set off for the shops. A rather grubby beige coloured thing it was, full of mysterious stamps, and carefully-noted details always written using fountain pens. The first biros had yet to arrive. And when we got to the shops, having navigated the unmade road that ran past them, even a child could sense there was not a lot to buy. I never enjoyed going in the fishmongers. They seemed to sell nothing except bright yellow haddock whose very sight put me off eating any fish at all. Something else I could not abide was cheese, which was always rock hard and smelt like unwashed socks.

No doubt the war, and the difficult years before it when money had been short for big families like the Owens and Frisbys, encouraged a frugal approach to food, and much else. Anything put in front of me had to be eaten. Even peas, which I really loathed. Interestingly, it was in the fairly authoritarian house run by Grandma Owen that I was never made to eat anything I did not care for. 'If you don't like peas,' she would say, 'I can't see the point of giving them to you.' I loved her, and all my grandparents, so very much. One of the immense joys of getting near old age is to enjoy grandchildren. And indulge them in a way you never would your own children. I bet my Dad when he was lad had to eat up everything, whatever his dislikes.

If money was always tight – and many times I saw my father count out the housekeeping in pound notes, and declare that was all the cash available – there were sometimes what must have been expensive treats. Like the time when I was aboard a grey airport coach, headed for an overseas holiday. It seems extraordinary now that when summer breaks could never be taken for granted – 'We can't afford a holiday this year,' I often heard Dad say – we went one summer to Guernsey. I was four years old. Heathrow airport was still being knocked together. Our coach took us to Northolt, and we flew in a Viscount, me strapped in on my father's knee. There is a picture of me brandishing a small windmill on a stick. I can't remember the windmill. I do remember slipping and falling headlong into some water as I ran too fast down a slope on to a beach. On another occasion, on a day trip to somewhere like Littlehampton, I stuck my head through the railings on an esplanade, leaned out too far, and fell onto hard ground below. Blows to the head seemed awfully frequent when I was a small boy.

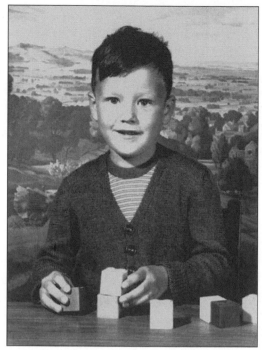

Five years old. Butter wouldn't melt . . .

By 1952 my parents had moved from the small terraced house in Selsdon to a pint-sized bungalow a few miles away in Sanderstead. I started school at Hamsey Green Primary. Getting there and back meant crossing a busy road. One afternoon Mum was late collecting me from the school gate. Maybe it was one of the many days when she felt ill. I set off home on my own . . . straight across the busy road. I hope I looked carefully. I rounded the last corner before the bungalow, and there Mum was, white with shock that this five-year-old had found his own way.

An adventure too far came a few weeks later. This time it wasn't my head that got injured. I fell awkwardly during playtime, and broke my left arm. After a trip in an ambulance, bell clanging, the arm was set at a hospital in Purley. I was six weeks with a sling. And a couple more weeks learning to use the arm again. Standing in the kitchen, supper finished, 'Journey Into Space' on the radio, my dad would be urging me to straighten that healed arm.

In 1953 the first television set arrived, bought by my parents in time for the Coronation, as so many people did. I was prancing around the garden with a shopping basket on my arm as the delivery man struggled in with his big, mysterious parcel of wood and electronics. The modern media world had come to Sanderstead. I remember the man and the delivery quite clearly. Better than the Coronation itself. Only one grainy TV sequence of the big royal day has stayed in my memory. The gorgeous golden coach came swaying past a camera with the young Queen and Prince Philip waving away at the crowds gathered in the relentless drizzle. Gold didn't make any impression in black and white. And as for the rain . . . well, it certainly made the picture pretty fuzzy.

The Coronation is one of two memories that are about the only historical qualifications I could claim when I became a TV Royal Correspondent in the 1990s. I remember the year before, standing by my mother's ironing board and asking her why the radio had gone all solemn music. 'Nicholas, the King is dead,' she said.

Mother's bouts of serious illness were frequent. When I was a toddler and she had been sick I had been sent to stay with my Uncle Jack and another Auntie Joan, my mother's younger sister. They lived just after the war in houses they rented on farms near Stoke on Trent. Like my Dad, Jack Louch had been in the Navy, and his first civilian work was with social services in Staffordshire.

The summer when I lost my mother I had been sent to stay with Uncle

My suave artist uncle Eric.

15

*Family: Auntie Joan, who told me of mum's death, extreme left; me extreme right.
Mother behind me, with only weeks to live. 1955.*

Eric and the other Joan in their house buried in the Sussex countryside at the village of Maplehurst. There were two things I loved about it. The huge back garden rambled on and on, with endless places to walk and scurry and hide. It was cowboy and Indian country, with me playing all the parts. And my uncle being a commercial artist had a studio in a large, airy room upstairs. It was so enjoyable to go in amid the pencils, crayons, pens, brushes, paints and expensive-smelling paper.

What an exotic way to earn a living. Eric looked the part too, with his goatee beard and a mane of black hair swept off a high forehead. He had suffered a problem with a hip from birth and always walked with a pronounced limp. Maybe the inconvenience explained his yen for fast cars. He had a sporty open-top AC and later a succession of Volkswagen Beetles, always driven at breakneck pace. Quite unlike chugging sedately and unreliably around in father's Morris Ten. Eric collected lots of speeding tickets in the easier-going days before penalty points on the licence made disqualification a distinct danger. Auntie Joan was a boisterous driver too. In her case, it was at the wheel of a smart green Morris Minor Traveller. I could just see over the dashboard as we darted along the winding country lanes. To Joan would fall the hardest of tasks. To tell me about my mother.

FOUR

Jack Bucknall was fanatical about cleaning teeth, his own and everyone else's. He was the energetic, youthful headmaster of Tavistock Hall, a preparatory school for boys nestling in the East Sussex countryside on the edge of the village of Heathfield. In the 1950s there were lots of similar schools dotted around rural England, run on spartan lines, with a disparate collection of staff, and pupils whose parents were often abroad somewhere, running a British colony, or in the Army. The scenes can so easily be re-played as film or television drama. The 1950s prep school, with all the period feel you can stomach: eccentric teachers, boys fat, thin, stupid, brainy. And never quite enough to eat.

It was not a cruel place. To me, however, it meant the most painful of separations from the world I knew, an experience made immensely more doleful by the recent loss of my mother. But what was a lad from a not very well-off family doing there anyway?

The complications of what happened after my mother's death were mostly invisible to a shellshocked boy of eight. The key to it all lay with my father's employment. Having come out of the Navy in 1945 he worked first for Legal and General, the insurance company. After a few years, he changed to a job in the City, with the merchant bank Rothschilds. They were a byword for paternalism. Not great payers, but great lookers-after. So when 35-year-old Tom Owen's wife died, leaving him with a young lad to bring up, the Rothschild bosses took a firm view. The boy would have to go away to school. I have often thought how disastrous a decision that would be thought today. I have no real clue how my Dad felt about it. Remembering his gentle, loving nature I imagine he hated the whole thing. But go I did.

My father could not bear to be in the bungalow he and mother had shared in Sanderstead. So he and I were billeted with good friends who had been neighbours when my parents got their first house. Auntie Kath and Uncle Rodney they would always be to me: the rescuers of Owen senior and Owen junior in their hour of extreme need. They made space first in their small Selsdon home, then in a bigger one they moved to in South Croydon. Bigger, but it needed to be. Kath and Rodney Dew had two daughters, Pat and Jackie, and a son Anthony, almost my own age and my oldest friend. He eventually became a gifted craftsman, designing and making the most beautiful rocking horses. So there were the five Dews, plus the two of us. Dad and I shared one small bedroom. It must have been quite a squeeze.

The Dews were our saviours. It was the most striking example of friendship that brought our families together, at the worst of times. Pat and Jackie were delightful company for a young boy: big sisters when affection was in short supply. One shivery delight was to sit and listen as Pat told ghost stories in that tall old South Croydon house. After them, I would creep, fairly terrified, up several flights of stairs to the bedroom which was home for father and me.

In September 1955 I had briefly exchanged Hamsey Green Primary school for another, bigger state school. It was a thoroughly intimidating place. Much, much worse was to follow. I was told that I would no longer be an ordinary pupil at an ordinary school. I was to become a boarder. The ghastliness of it petrified me. How ever loving my one parent, it was not a time when a small boy's cries and pleas would have carried a lot of weight. Dad himself had six years of war and serious injury in his own recent past.

To describe a parent's character and personality is one of the greatest difficulties facing anyone trying to set the 'real' person down in words. You can quote what they said. You can say what they looked like. Altogether harder is trying to separate complicated emotions jumbled up with faded memories. Until recently I would have said, fairly simply, that he was a reserved, shy man. His sister, my Auntie Barbara, tells me he went away to the Second World War the cheery extrovert; he came back after seeing so many frightful things and suffering serious injury a changed and quieter man. I have his wartime diaries. I can see why the ordeals he endured changed him forever. His Rothschild superiors told the ex-Navy man that boarding school was the right solution. Twenty-first-century notions of emoting and expressing feelings would have been unthinkable. Chins had to be up. No good weeping. Worse things were always happening at sea. It was one of Tom Owen's favourite phrases, and such a personally-felt one in his case. My father was a City man, but never a wealthy one. The school would be expensive. The bank would pay the fees, for a while at any rate.

The pain and dislocation of being sent away were intensified by happening half-way through that first autumn term following Mother's death, when one strange school was replaced by a much stranger one. Tavistock Hall was approached up a long driveway that swung first left and then right between high rhododendrons. The drive opened up in a sweep of gravel at the front of a large house. To its right was a bungalow, home to some of the teachers. To the left of the house, and wrapped round behind it, were the shed-like classrooms.

Headmaster Jack Bucknall's study was just to the left of the main house's front door. There are fleeting recollections of him and my father greeting each other after our arrival, the head booming away about the virtues of the school, with promises to look out for me, as cheerful smiles were beamed in my direction. Some of my belongings came in a wooden box, with my name – Nicholas D.A. Owen – in thick black letters. Nowadays, it's a useful toy box in my daughter's home. My grandchildren happily play around it, so blissfully unaware of the dark memories it conjures for me. At Tavistock, the box was dragged away and piled up with others in a corridor smelling of damp overcoats and musty shoes.

Some of the rest of that first boarding school day are engraved on memory. Sitting in the dining hall at the back of the big house, I watched a bright red evening sun sliding slowly down a window. I stared through the glass, thinking of the vast distance between the school and my father, driving back in the wheezy old Morris, getting further and further away and leaving me no prospect of escaping back home. Even if home was that cramped room at Kath and Rodney's. Someone suggested I write a letter to Dad. I spilled out my misery, and my hatred of the alien surroundings. The letter was returned to me. 'You don't want to upset your father, do you?' A pared-down, cleaned-up, jollied-up version was put together. I like to imagine my father would have seen through the plucky words, and guessed at the nightmare. Still, worse things happen at sea . . .

And speaking of nightmares, some of the worst times would come at night. The dormitories were shared with about ten other boys. They knew each other well, and all about the school, its ways and its customs. Lying in a room full of strangers, as a teacher trod past the door and flicked off the light outside, was hell for a boy afraid of the dark, along with all the other horrors life had produced. Daytime and the bullies could be horrible too. Amazing how names come floating back after more than half a century. Where is one of my old Tavistock Hall mates, a Mr Tate (perhaps Tait) now? He was all of ten years old, gangly and rough. His two years' seniority meant he got the pleasure of giving me not just a few thumps but usually a good kicking too. He tended to choose that smelly corridor where my school box was kept, where he was unlikely to be interrupted by any of the staff.

The food was not very varied nor very enjoyable. Doubtless the fees were not all that high, and economy measures extended to the kitchen. Kippers were flat and leathery. Curry was bright yellow. There would be piles of blackish bread on each long table in the dining hall. You had to take each slice from the pile as you came to it. No diving in to pick out the occasional, enticing white one which hungry eyes would spot the moment you took your place. One oddity was that anyone having a birthday would be allowed the crusts carefully cut from the nearest teacher's white toast. What a treat!

Sunday nights meant two things: cheese and films. There would be a knob of cheddar with supper, then we would troop into the hall for some movies. A travelling projectionist would set up his kit, and I would munch away on that precious chunk of mousetrap, illegally pocketed at the dining table. Two of the films I loved, and I prayed for their constant re-appearance. One was a colour feature by the Shell film unit, all about volcanoes and the wonderful rivers of red and yellow fire that poured from them. The other was *San Francisco*, the story of the 1906 earthquake. It was a black and white Hollywood masterpiece, at least in the opinion of an enthralled eight-year-old.

Sunday night at the movies was a place to forget unhappiness for a while. There were some other good things to enjoy. Long romps through the woods that adjoined the school grounds. Rolling in bracken, splashing along muddy and rutted pathways, and confrontations with 'village boys', lucky youngsters who actually had homes to go to in the evenings and at weekends.

There was one magical place in the woods. It was a bridge over the single track railway that brought steam trains to Heathfield from London. Sometimes that was how I travelled to the school. It was a beautiful country branch line that Dr Beeching killed off in the 1960s. The ancient trains struggled round the sharp curves, up and down the steep gradients, and through the black tunnels. Very often the carriage lights failed to come on, and I would stare into the pitch dark, terrified that my sight would never return.

The school staff were a varied crew. Bucknall was brisk, never more so than first in the morning, vigorously slashing a toothbrush round his mouth, emphasising to wide-eyed new boys that this was an essential for good health. A teacher called Wyman had been a soldier in the First World War. He had one artificial leg, but that was no bar to him reviving his parade ground ways and getting us outside good and early, drilling shivering boys in flimsy vests on icy mornings.

Another, much younger man had his two legs, but was whispered to have only one lung. He would be kind to me. Between the holidays, there would be 'exeats', one day at a weekend when parents – single parent in my case – would take you out. Dad and I would usually slope down to Eastbourne, some dozen miles away on the coast. Father was never religious as such. I was later to hear him whispering to my stepmother, in answer to a question from her, that he did not believe in an afterlife. Yet I remember in Eastbourne he took me to church services that were not just Anglican, but of the High variety. Lots of incense and curious wailing amid the prayers and hymns. Perhaps a spiritual need had followed the death of his young wife. Much more fun were the open-top bus rides along the promenade and up to Beachy Head.

One exeat weekend, my father did not appear. I waited and waited, watching from a front window of the school as car after car arrived to take other boys to Eastbourne, or wherever. After some phone calls, it turned out my parent was ill, and couldn't come. Mr one-lung sat beside my bed that night, chatting softly as, wretched, I tried to sleep. Much less kindness came from Mr Edwards, a burly, ill-tempered man who seemed to me quite elderly. He glared a great deal, especially at those, like me, who had difficulty with his subject, maths. Just about the best aspect of leaving Tavistock eventually would be saying goodbye to this martinet. Did I say goodbye? Fate would surprise on that score.

Work was an antidote to brooding. I discovered a love of a subject that most youngsters tolerated and quite a few loathed. I did terrifically well at Latin, a language I would never have gone near if I had not been despatched to private school. Latin and subjects like English and History, plus the film shows and getting away now and then to wander the woods, became happy interludes in that isolated existence. They meant the bullying, the food, the early morning drills, and Edwards and his maths, could just about be tolerated.

And there was the story-telling. Dormitory life was an ordeal, as I've said, especially for a new bug like me. Especially one with a home life that was a wreck. I made a discovery that has been stumbled on by other lonely lads in boarding schools. Did it not occur in *Tom Brown's*

Schooldays, that classic that I read years afterwards to send shivers down my spine, to remind me of my own bad experiences away at school? Or somewhere among Dickens's downtrodden creatures?

The discovery was that unhappiness could be deflected by story-telling. It turned out that I could spin yarns after lights-out that were so popular they became a nightly demand from my colleagues. More than that, somehow the information that I could tell a story, and certainly read one, spread to the headmaster and his wife. I would sometimes be extracted from the 'dorm', and sent to read and talk to the head's own small children.

Sometimes real life intruded on our remote little world. For someone who ended up as a journalist, the third hint of a big story breaking somewhere – remembering that the first and second were the death of George VI and the Coronation of his daughter – came at Tavistock Hall during assembly one morning in 1956. 'Boys,' Jack Bucknall announced, 'we are at war with Egypt.'

It was the Suez crisis, probably the foreign adventure that really told the world Britain was no longer the force of Empire she had been. To me, it was a new nightmare. War? Did that mean my father would be back in that uniform, and maybe never come back from somewhere or other? Here is a fact about losing a parent when you are young. You spend an awful lot of time terrified that you are going to lose the other as well.

One curiosity about father was that although he had been in the Navy, he did not swim. I think there had been an old maritime superstition that the ability to do so was unnatural, and somehow you were more likely to end up overboard. Someone in charge at Tavistock Hall decided I should be taught. Their idea of instruction was to ignore my pleas not to go anywhere near the water. I was picked up, and thrown in a pool. The memory of sinking fast, of bubbles spilling out of my mouth and up into my hair, of my complete panic, has never left me. I learned to swim, very poorly, in my forties. Give me a nice outdoor pool, and I'll probably go in. I can even swim under the surface. Just don't ask me to do anything out of my depth.

I never much enjoyed football, and played rugby only once to acquire a lifelong aversion. I did get to enjoy cricket and athletics. A stringy kid, I turned out to be an excellent sprinter. The school's 100-yard champion in due course. A lifetime later I still tend to dart around.

The day came when father arrived, probably for an exeat, accompanied by a woman. A little younger than him, she was very attractive, and she worked at Rothschilds too. Cautiously, my Dad introduced me to Diana Hawxwell. I liked her. It was just as well. At the start of one of the holidays, my father drove Diana and me to a village in Surrey, not too far from where we had lived with my mother. Most of the houses in Kingswood were large affairs, with sweeping driveways and lush gardens. One cul-de-sac had more modest properties. When Kingswood was being laid out as a posh commuter haven in the early 1900s, Drive Spur was where the artisans' more modest homes were built, coming first so that there was labour on site to work on the mansions.

Dad and I got out of the car at the top of the hilly cul de sac. As we wandered down it, he asked what I would think if we were to live there. And furthermore, what would I think were he to marry Diana? I thought it a good plan, particularly as he followed up his second question by saying they would like to marry soon so that I could be brought home from boarding school. It took some time, but I did get to call her 'Mummy'. And she is my mother in all the pages that follow. I didn't go to their wedding. It was some years before I heard tales that my father's quite sophisticated family – remember Grandma and her insistence on smart appearance and proper speech – found the Hawxwell people, some of them anyway, rather 'different'. The reception in Streatham, south London, must have been an interesting event. Pity I wasn't invited.

A couple of postscripts. A few years back, I went to see Jack Bucknall's widow, and meet some of her grown-up children to whom I had read stories. The ever-active Jack had died at about 80 after a vigorous squash game. Mrs Bucknall, very charming and most gracious as we had tea at her home in Hove, said after we'd talked of those long-gone days: 'You seem to have flourished.' Kind of her to put it so nicely. As I have made clear, Tavistock was not a shocker of a school, not a grim place in the way Rugby was for my fictional soul-mate Tom Brown. No doubt being wrenched away from home after my mother's death had toughened up a little boy, and perhaps made the adult more determined to find some sort of distinctive way in life. No hard feelings, Jack.

I had seen the man himself once, long after leaving his care. I had started work as a newspaper reporter. The drive up through the rhododendrons still made me uneasy, the large school house still made me want to turn and flee. Old dark fears were tempered by curiosity and the strange elation of knowing I could leave at any moment I chose. In I went, turning left to talk to my old headmaster in his study. He clearly could not recall the boy who, after all, had only been a pupil for a couple of years.

What class were you in, he asked. Who else was there? I remembered some names. One made him light up. 'Ah, yes. Smythe!' Smythe had made a real impact. Not for any scholarly achievements. He had gone on to be a croupier at a London casino. And Jack Bucknall had been up to town as Smythe's guest on one occasion. *There* was an old boy to be proud of . . .

FIVE

Boarding school may have been left behind, to my great relief. Private education had a little longer to run. If there were many Tavistock Halls, there were also a lot of day preparatories like St Christopher's. It was about a mile from our new home in Kingswood, close to the shops and the station. And it was just as set in its 1950s ways as the establishment down in East Sussex. The headmaster was another who could have been from central casting. Instead of the tall, sprightly figure of Jack Bucknall, who enjoyed sliding down the banisters at Heathfield, Major Clare was short, moved slowly, wore a tweed suit, and liked to quote Latin.

Perhaps he'd seen a report remarking on my enjoyment and progress with the language. As my newly-married parents and I sat in his study, he peered over his half moons and said: 'Education. It comes from the Latin. Nicholas, what does *duco* mean?'

'I lead,' I said proudly.

'Exactly. And the *"e"* means out of. Education is to lead out of someone the skills that they have.'

I was rather impressed with the Major. Mother and father probably thought him an old-fashioned fart.

Leading out my skills meant going to and from the school five and a half days a week, to have more of the beloved Latin, other subjects like English, History and Geography which I enjoyed, and Maths, which I still did not. Saturday mornings were annoyingly cluttered with arithmetic, geometry and algebra. Very little was led out of me from that trio. At the start of my second term at St Christopher's came disaster. We were gathered for the first assembly. Major Clare, his bearing enhanced a bit by a flowing black gown, announced that we were to be joined by a new maths master. Feelings of doom came easily to a boy by now ten who'd had more than his fair share of setbacks. The headmaster was waving towards the back of the hall, inviting his new employee to come forward. I swivelled round. Could it be? It *was*. The feared Edwards,

26

who had done much to add to my miseries of boarding, had found a new job.

I had told my father of my strong dislike and even fear of the man. Maybe in some circuitous way Edwards had got to hear that I was among his new pupils. And that my parents were only a mile or so away. Whatever changed him, his behaviour was a good deal less severe towards me. That did nothing to make my grasp of mathematics any better. And a lot of the boys disliked the new master as much as I had done at Tavistock. Which brought me a moment of glory. Curiously, it was on the cricket field. Cricket, as I've said, was one sport I liked, and was even quite good at. Vague dreams of playing for England even danced around my head when I managed to knock out a dozen or two runs, or take a handful of wickets.

One day, Edwards, built on brick shithouse lines, was square leg umpire, planted like an angry-looking statue in a long white coat some 20 yards behind the batsman's back. When it was my turn to bat, I faced bowling I was confident I could deal with. The bowler padded towards me, the ball bounced once, and came at just the right angle. I swept a firm shot right round and away over my left shoulder. Right at the hated Edwards. The ball actually went straight towards his head.

At the last possible moment, his hands still wedged in the pockets of his white coat, he eased the top of his big body to the right. The ball flew past his left ear. I was the school hero: the Boy who Nearly Killed Old Edwards. I like to think there are at least a couple among the 22 who played that summer afternoon who still remember such a feat of sporting arms.

Heading my way about the same time was trouble I could not have foreseen. I was to take the eleven plus examination. Everyone had to sit it. Nice little prep schools like St Christopher's took children from five to thirteen, when they would sit their Common Entrance exam to take them on to public school. Their privileged youngsters were almost all destined to be wafted up to Charterhouse, Shrewsbury, Winchester, or some such desirable destination. Well-off parents would continue to pay for the smooth journey that is private education. The trouble for me was that somewhere along the line my father's bank had decided that funding *my* education was an expense they no longer wished to bear. Therefore, unprepared, I sat through a hot couple of days a few miles away in a state school, staring bewildered at examination papers I'd never seen the like of before. The school was in Picquets – always pronounced 'Picketts' – Way, Banstead.

I failed the exam. So I ended a summer term in the rarefied and reasonably congenial atmosphere of St Christopher's, to start in September at a very different place. During those perspiring two days of exams I had been so glad Picquet's Way was not my school. As with Edwards revisited, fate had decided on another mean trick. Flunking the eleven plus meant that was precisely where I was now going. I learned later that parents of St Christopher's boys would threaten their little darlings with attendance there, if academic ideas were not bucked up. I had not been threatened. Money was short so I ended up in the large State secondary anyway.

Many older people nowadays hanker after some misty vision of a golden age of schooling when discipline was real. When teachers were feared. When children sat in obedient rows and digested gratefully dollops of information, be it about the Iron Age, the capital of Tanganyika, the intricacies of Pythagoras, the glories of Dickens ... or whatever.

Some of that was true, half a century ago. Teachers could certainly be feared. I found myself on day one at Picquets Way sitting among about forty boys – rather than the twenty or less at St Christopher's – being given a rundown of the school's routine by a master who was said to have been in one of the Guards regiments. He was tall, spare, with a pencil moustache and thinning hair. He never smiled.

As he explained how our days would be organised, the door of the classroom opened, and two dishevelled youths edged nervously in, glancing with great apprehension at the ex-Guardsman. I have mentioned learning of the glories of Charles Dickens's work. These lads could certainly have stepped from his pages. They looked ill-fed and ill-kempt. They came from a residential establishment for boys who were victims of what were then called 'broken homes'. Today such homes seem almost in the majority. Beechholme was not far from the school, and it was another old-fashioned institution long since buried under suburban redevelopment.

In the 21st century, all sorts of reasons for the boys' hopeless appearance would be advanced. Especially their deprived backgrounds. Society would be at fault. In 1958 no-one I knew thought like that. Most Beechholme boys were considered quite straightforwardly, and probably very often unfairly, as thieving toe rags. The two now gazing with increasing concern at our ex-Guardsman had been caught pinching something or other. 'So, you've been stealing again,' said the teacher quietly as he got up from his desk. He moved a couple of steps towards them. And beat them up.

Forty eleven-year-old boys, 'A' streamers, so rather more than sensitive than some of their contemporaries in the 'B' and 'C' streams might have been, watched aghast as the six foot-plus schoolmaster delivered a few swift blows that had the pair sprawled on the floor, noses bleeding. 'Get out. Don't let me catch you again.' They heaved to their feet, and fled. Welcome to the world of State education in the days when Prime Minister Harold Macmillan was assuring everyone that we had 'never had it so good.' What he actually said was that *most* people had never had it so good. Beechholme boys and the like had always had it bad.

That was brutality. Most of us never experienced anything like it, although corporal punishment was dished out regularly. The headmaster, 'Chewy' Spearing, reserved the right to use the cane. All teachers wielded the slipper. Bent over in front of your classmates, you could never quite prepare yourself for just how painful a rubbery old plimsoll could be. Your eyes would sting with tears. The desperation was always to prevent actual tears rolling down your cheeks. Yet to be slippered gave you a certain cachet among your mates. You swaggered for the rest of the day, even if your buttocks twinged with the fiery reminder of the moment of punishment. In the 21st century, most adults seem horrified that out-of-control teenagers regard Anti-Social Behaviour Orders (ASBOs) as badges of honour. I am not at all surprised.

There was no more Latin. My maths was deteriorating. Metalwork and carpentry were grimy mysteries to me. Other subjects, especially English and History, were taught well, and I was always near the top of the class come the end of term. Football was to be dodged. Cricket was still to be enjoyed, though my enthusiasm and skill were on the wane.

There were two schools in Picquets Way, and they shared a large playing field. In the middle was a huge oak tree. It was the dividing line between two worlds that were deliberately kept apart, yet to which each side was drawn with increasing interest as the years went by. Beyond the tree was the girls' secondary school. As I approached 13, some of the boys, the bigger ones, began to take more and more notice of the other half of the field it was forbidden to cross. I was among the hangers-back, fascinated, and dreadfully uninformed.

Another academic hurdle loomed. There was recognition then that the eleven plus could disadvantage the young and unprepared. So there was another chance, a safety net of an examination called the thirteen plus. It was based on coursework, and if the examiners turned a bit of a blind eye to my maths, everything else was pretty good. Pass, and a grammar school place was available. I got through. The question was where I would go next. A list was sent to my parents. My father was very much in favour of Caterham School, a refined, public school-like outfit. Something deeply 'anti' was in me, maybe a legacy of my own unhappy private education days. I picked a place where grammar classes ran alongside lesser lights. West Ewell Secondary Modern was not only quite a long way from where we lived, it also entailed an awkward journey. Therein lay its great attraction. For a lad who loved trains and buses, it would mean a fiddly journey by both. Many would recoil from the inconvenience. I would love it.

West Ewell was definitely a cut above Picquets Way. A couple of the masters swished around in the academic gowns I had not seen since St Christopher's. Mr Thomas, a large red-faced Welshman, taught English. He was rather a pain, but his subject was my delight. Mr Thorburn was short and menacing. He was in charge of mathematics. We did not get on.

The job now was to move towards GCE 'O' (for 'Ordinary') levels, the equivalent of today's GCSEs. Because the thirteen plus meant pupils like me were effectively a year behind those clever passers of the eleven plus, I would not sit my O levels till I was 17. Hormones, some deep laziness, an urge to get shot of school and go to work – had not my Dad and his brothers left, fully educated, at 14? – gradually eroded my classroom attention. I scraped five O levels eventually, having a couple of years earlier given up arithmetic, geometry, and algebra altogether, an unheard-of bit of cowardice that I am amazed was tolerated. Curiously, later in life I was adept with figures, highly useful for someone who would report on high finance for more than a decade. Unsurprisingly, the geometric theorems and algebraic puzzles which had always baffled me so utterly never did come in handy.

There was a curious bump along the GCE road. A few months before the summertime exams, we sat the 'mocks'. I had shed the dreaded Maths, was doing passably well at the rest, although French and Physics were dire. By some devious means, the mock Physics paper fell into unethical hands before the exam. I had plenty of time to scurry about and find the answers. When the mock results came out, I along with other Physics duffers got wonderfully high marks. There must have been strong suspicions. No doubt the teachers thought, what the hell. Nemesis would come. And so it did. I took seven GCEs and failed two, and failed them badly. French and, of course, Physics. Even so, the total of five subjects passed would turn out to be important.

I never attended another class at my West Ewell Secondary from the day of the last examination. One disappointment was to discover that the English master, Mr Thomas, took no pride in learning what I had decided to do in life. I went back once to West Ewell when it was still a secondary school and sought him out. I expected him to be pleased that his English teaching had led to what I hoped would be a lifetime of journalism. A writer, you could say. He turned away, totally uninterested. I suppose he had the average person's low estimation of my wonderful trade.

Before I was finished with school, the world beyond the Picquets Way oak tree began to intrude. My first date was with a girl who was at the West Ewell school. We went one afternoon to the Rembrandt cinema at Stoneleigh. I drive past where it used to be frequently these days, and always glance at the apartments that were built on the site when the film shows ended. I took the girl to see *Summer Holiday*. I was sure she would love Cliff Richard and the Shadows in all their young glory. And I was eager to see the London bus that was at the heart of the story of a cheerful, tuneful gang who flee dreary old England for a holiday in Greece: 'We're going where the sun shines brightly ... we're going where the sea is blue ...'

The sun, the singing, and the bus were all there. Mutual attraction was not. Outside the cinema, I planted a quick kiss on her cheek, and that was the last romantic moment together. She 'chucked' me, as we used to say. I was so miserable. Only very recently, a friend wondered if I had behaved, shall we say, immoderately in the darkness as the movie progressed. Oh no, I said, not at all. Ah, he wondered further, maybe that was what had disappointed her.

A couple of years ago, I wrote a few articles for a magazine called *Caribbean World*. I interviewed famous folk who had connections with those parts. That highest of high-profile West Indians Sir Trevor McDonald was an early and obvious choice. Another star who I met at his management company's office near where I live in Surrey was Sir Cliff Richard, who had a holiday home in Barbados. As we ended I told him of the time I saw *Summer Holiday*. I blame you, I joked, for losing me that first girl friend. He was kind enough to laugh. I was kind enough not to mention that I have never had any desire to go to Barbados, or any part of the Caribbean.

SIX

My father was a difficult man to know. His attitude to religion, for one thing. I have already said that he did not believe there was anything after death. Yet he had a spiritual life of some sort. There had been those bewildering, incense-choked high church moments in Eastbourne during boarding school days. And as a lad in the drowsy village of Kingswood, I was ordered to take religion seriously. For a while I had to walk two miles or more each way every Sunday to the plain Anglican services at St Andrew's Church. I had a suit only worn that day, a heavy grey number that was always uncomfortable and smelt strongly of dry cleaning fluid.

The St Andrew's services did not appeal much at all. Then I was switched to the Crusaders, which met at Picquets Way school on Sundays. Enthusiastic young bible teachers tried to get a roomful of mostly reluctant boys to take an interest in the great achievements of Jesus's life and ministry. Much later on, when George Bush Junior was in the White House, the expression 'Crusade' stirred hostile reactions among many Muslims. It sometimes sounded as if old mediaeval wars of religion were being re-fought. In the late 1950s, at Picquets Way on Sunday mornings, none of those nagging issues surfaced. No doubts were voiced about the spreading of our Saviour's message as we belted out the old hymns. Often we lads were in trouble for modifying them. 'I will make you fishers of men' ran one rousing line. Which we would invariably convert to 'I will make you vicious old men.'

'Stop ... stop!' the young preacher at the wheezy little organ would shout. 'Start again. And make sure you sing the words as they were written.' What beastly blasphemers we were.

In order to instil the ways of the Lord into us there was a trip away to a big rambling house on the Isle of Wight for a heavy dose of Crusading. I was to be distinctly unimpressed. A bright-eyed and quite charismatic youth leader told us he wanted us to declare ourselves for The Lord. Not just that, but also to promise to be missionaries. You had to go to his room to make the final solemn commitment. 'And have you decided, Nicholas?' he said, placing a hand firmly, too firmly, on my knee. I retreated. I was very innocent, but very suspicious too. Like father, I had not been persuaded to believe in an afterlife, though the church and bible class experiences have at least left me with a lifelong love of singing hymns. Many of them I know by heart, thanks to those endless classes and services.

If Dad was a mystery when it came to praying and the rest, we agreed on one important aspect of life. It was not worthwhile without work. When I was fourteen, the age at which my father had left school, I got myself an early morning paper round. Newspapers were a lot lighter than they have become, but it was still a heck of a load to haul by bicycle around the hilly lanes of Kingswood village. I have never enjoyed getting up early. It was a miserable job for the equivalent of little more than 50 pence a week. My early love affair with newspapers faltered badly when I struggled with those papers through the notoriously bad winter of 1963. One icy and dark early morning, the bike tipped over and I was left stranded like a turtle on its back, the sack of newspapers on top of me, almost too heavy to move.

I earned a few more 'bob', as we called shillings – one shilling being the equivalent today of five pence – helping out sometimes on a milk round. Slippery, slimy milk bottles could be dodgy to handle when it was freezing cold, as it always seemed to be. Everyone had milk delivered then, and so it was stop and start along the plush lanes of Kingswood. And stop and start in electric milk floats. In 2007, I bought my first hybrid petrol plus electric car – how green of me – and I often think of those little milk vans with their electric motors whining and straining up the village's steep hills.

Another and better paying part-time job was to caddy at the local and very posh golf club. Seven and sixpence a round (32½ pence) you could get for dragging some snooty man's clubs around. A great memory was seeing at the club Douglas Bader, the World War Two fighter pilot famous for his tin legs, the legacy of a pre-war accident. He took part in a charity match, standing all square with pipe clenched in his teeth, every inch the fighter ace who was a national hero. One of the great British golfers, Tony Jacklin, took part in the same match.

A less happy memory was caddying one blazing summer day when the two golfers I was trailing came to the ninth hole where a little drinks trolley had been set up. Under a wide umbrella, the two players got their refreshment from a flunky wearing a white jacket. And the caddy? I was left standing out in the very hot sunshine, no drink offered. It gave me a dislike of golf and golfers that took years to overcome. And the incident undoubtedly made me quite 'chippy' about snobby people who fail to notice the discomforts of others.

I trailed once behind two middle-aged members. One asked the other: 'Wasn't it your birthday yesterday?'

'Yes.'

'Happy returns. Um . . . did you get your, you know, proper birthday present?'

'Oh yes!' They sauntered on, chuckling away. When I asked my mother later what they were on about, she blushed a wee bit, and affected to be mystified. A few more months would have to pass before I cottoned on.

After my less than glorious five GCEs I managed to get a summer job in the small supermarket in the parade of shops in Kingswood. I filled shelves and helped carry bags. I marvelled at the older staff, some married, who could put up with such humdrum work for years on end. One day at the bacon counter a customer watched me at work. 'You know,' she said, 'you really should get yourself a proper apprenticeship with someone like Sainsbury's.' There was a thought chillier than the shop's refrigerator cabinets. I had no intention of being a lifelong retailer. My absolute determination was to be a newspaper reporter.

Here is a question so often asked: what made you want to be a journalist? I think I owe it more to Grandad Frisby than anyone, or anything, else. Tom Frisby, and his life so different from my other, more staid grandparents. After the optical trade, my grandfather spent 20 years or more at the *Daily Worker*, the communist newspaper, eventually to be renamed the *Morning Star*. He was a never a communist himself. It would be hard to imagine a man from a largish house in the tranquil suburb of Beckenham ever being an agitator for revolutionary change. If one puzzle was why he should be at the *Worker*, another was exactly what he *did*. He was not a journalist. I always had the impression he was a sort of doorkeeper. For much of the 20th century, national papers, even minority-taste ones like the *Daily Worker*, employed a lot of folk whose jobs could be quite imprecise. His newspaper was not in Fleet Street, but round the corner in the Farringdon Road. That did not stop it bumping along with the same dubious employment practices that bedevilled the 'street of ink' itself. Perhaps its Soviet paymasters thought they were doing their bit to provide jobs for the downtrodden British working class.

Downtrodden or not, most interesting to his young grandson were Tom's working hours. My Frisby grandparents had a large dresser cluttered with ornate cups, saucers, plates and knick-knacks collected on various holidays. Propped up in a corner was a card which detailed Tom's rota. He came and went at all manner of hours: some days there would be a ludicrously early start; at other times he would be heading for Farringdon Road in mid-afternoon.

It was so wonderfully unlike the predictable nine-to-five existence of most of the adults I knew. Newspapers must be thrillingly different places, I thought. Once I got to about ten, I started designing newspaper front pages. And reading the real ones voraciously. One year at Picquets Way, that school for the mainly unacademic, we were set a general knowledge exam. I came out way, way ahead of everyone else. If I could have remembered the adjective for someone from Cornwall, I would have scored 100 per cent.

Journalism began its mating cry in my direction. It was aided and abetted by someone who has remained among my oldest friends. Peter Denton was a few years ahead of me at Picquets Way. Indeed he was invested with some authority, being a prefect who sometimes took charge of my class. No school was ever rash enough to make me a prefect. Peter got into journalism very young, contributing stuff about school life to the local paper. Leaving at fifteen, he joined the same paper, and stayed writing happily for it for nine years.

I wanted to do the same. One problem was objections at home to my declared choice of job. Not, you may notice, choice of *career*. That is a word I think you can never apply to journalism. It is a delightfully random way of earning a living. I know the world is full now of media courses. The truth remains that journalism can never be about a string of qualifications. Professions have to set all sorts of rules entwined with barriers to make sure the untrained do not advance too far. Thankfully, a five O level boy stood as much chance as an Oxbridge graduate when it came getting and reporting the news. I happen to think the same principles should still apply today.

Peter Denton, impeccably smart and polite, was perfect to play an important role in winning over my sceptical mother. She had heard about reporters. Drunkenness and dubious sexual behaviour were rife, she knew. A neighbour had a relative who had spent a lifetime drifting from one less-than-brilliant weekly paper to another. I was not told whether he was also habitually drunk and an indulger in dubious sex. Knowing of

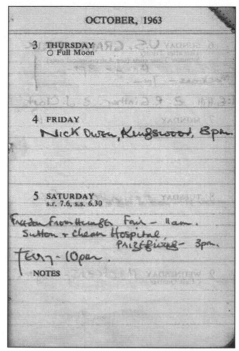

Key date: Peter Denton's diary. He came to talk about a job in journalism.

Peter's glorious leap from school straight into a reporter's chair I decided to ask my mother and father to invite him for dinner. I was sure he would paint a glowing picture of the fulfilling, even important, life of a newsroom. He did. He only spoiled the show slightly very near the end of the meal. In those days, even so-called 'professionals' like reporters were paid in cash. At the end of the week, journalists, printers and everyone else would be busy stripping open the little brown envelopes to see just how much they had made. Not a lot, as we shall soon learn. The temptation, Peter explained, was to do a bit of gambling when the pay packets came round. A card game often got started. He chortled as he talked of a colleague who went home one Friday with no cash at all after a run of poor luck. Mother's fears multiplied. To drinking and fornicating could be added the perils of the card tables.

Not that I had entirely ignored my Mum's apprehensions. I had vaguely considered other ways of earning a living. Loving books, for instance, meant that being a librarian sounded ok, if not very exciting. As with so many other jobs, there was much stress on starting at the proverbial bottom, working terribly hard, and earning precious little for ages. Probably forever if it was in a library. There was one delightful exception. In those days, advice on careers consisted of a few leaflets supposed to encourage you in the choice of a job. I looked at a few. One stood out: the one about advertising. It was obviously written by somebody who not only worked in the business, but also thoroughly enjoyed it. And had done well out of it. It talked of very jolly times at the office, little or no experience required, and a nice salary to go with it. My Uncle Eric clearly had a good time in advertising. Tempting. But newspapers had my heart.

Meanwhile, there was the job in the shop to be done. As well as the shelf-filling and the bacon slicing, there was the cleaning of the windows. It was a task I never really mastered. On a Monday morning, I would take bucket, soapy water, cloth and stepladder and try to make the big plate glass windows at the front of Roberts Stores nice and transparent. I would struggle not to leave any cloth marks. It seemed impossible to me. There were always streaks as the glass dried. My respect for window cleaners has never ceased since.

I would have loved to go out 'on the van'. These days deliveries from supermarkets to homes, working from orders sent in by customers over the Internet, are thought of as a modern retailing marvel. We were doing more or less the same half a century ago. My mother was one of those who would drop in a list of requirements, and the van would come round once a week. Sometimes, the big cardboard box would even contain almost everything that she had ordered. Not often. My Mum would be on the phone most weeks, complain about missing items, and the van would have to come out again.

The nearest I got to going on the round was helping to load the groceries. The driver could not have been much more than 25. Somehow, he managed to be raising a family on what must have been appallingly poor pay. He was incredulous that I should wish to work on a newspaper. Surely, he said, a newsroom would be a dreadfully *noisy* place? Yes, I said, failing to understand why that should be anything other than spice to the excitement. He shook his head, and drove off with his cardboard boxes to begin his deliveries.

Lacking any personal contacts, there was only one way I knew to get a job on a paper: to write to the editors of local ones. Four letters went out. I think two said sorry, not at the moment; one was lukewarm; one said come for a chat. Well, not a chat exactly. Hardly a word anyone would have used in 1964, and certainly not to describe any sort of meeting in an office. This was to be an interview with the

Editor, something very serious and petrifying for a shelf-filler with five O levels.

Cecil Gegg had been with the *Surrey Mirror*, based at Redhill a few miles from my home, since well before the Second World War. He commuted every day from his home in Dorking by steam train. I never saw him without his jacket on, and I would never, ever, have called him 'Cecil'. Mr Gegg gave me a job. I was seventeen. The salary was seven pounds five shillings (£7.25) a week. If I had got less than the five O levels I could still have made it. Except the rewards would have dropped to six pounds, fifteen shillings (£6.75).

One sharp lesson learned at that time about money concerned the shop. Everyone there, even my van driver friend, had wished me well as I went off one afternoon to my interview at the paper. They were all so pleased that I was accepted. However, when my pay slip came round a few days later, the amount of time I had been absent from Roberts Stores had been calculated down to the last minute, and a few precious shillings and pence had been deducted.

Newspapers were never to be that cheeseparing, although there was a formality pretty well unknown today. In spite of it, Cecil Gegg was a cheery and kindly Editor. Dotted down the years have been figures in journalism who have been great influences: he was the first. Several of his wise pieces of advice have stayed with me. Always be ready, he said, to interview a duchess or a dustman. I often think of that remark when I see remarkably unkempt reporters on the TV screen.

He advised taking the charitable view if you possibly can. A good example was an early theatre review I did. I was sent along to a local amateur production that was frankly ghastly. I had begun to do quite a bit of amateur acting myself by then – shades of my mother and father back in the 1930s – so I did have some clue as to what was really entertaining. I wrote a long, scorching piece, demolishing the cast and the whole production. Gegg called me in. He would run my review. It would however be cut right down. If you must be unkind, he said, keep it short. Again, I think of that when I read critics joyously ripping apart at length someone's hard artistic efforts.

Getting one's own name in a paper – getting a 'by-line' – was always an enormous thrill. Let me be honest. It is *still* a thrill to see anything published with 'Nicholas Owen' above it. In the 1960s, especially in the local Press, by-lines were extremely rare. Theatre reviews were an example where anonymity could be breached, but only by a set of initials at the end of the article. In my case the practice had a curiously negating effect on what I wrote. A piece full of what I hoped was useful information and insight would finish with 'NO' in bold type. A couple of full stops would have helped. I expect the sub editors enjoyed leaving them out.

By-lines or no by-lines, the duck took to water. I simply adored my local newspaper days.

SEVEN

The *Surrey Mirror* office was a strange, ramshackle affair. Because of a fire nine months before, the newspaper was making do. The reporters and the sub editors – the 'subs' wrote headlines and corrected copy – were based in a sort of prefabricated shed stuck on top of the printing works. My clothes soon started smelling of ink. Access to the shed was by way of an iron fire-escape staircase which became lethal when it rained. I twisted an ankle rushing down it once, and was in discomfort for weeks.

Those preparing the editorial and those printing it were literally on top of each other. There was a step in the middle of the process: once the copy was written and edited, it had to go elsewhere to be set into the metal type that would then come back to the print shop. Taking bundles of the subbed copy the two and a bit miles to where it was set meant a bus ride by the most junior reporter. And that responsibility brought me face to face with the challenges of that hallowed journalistic occupation: working out your expenses. The pay of £7.25 a week, minus a smidgeon of tax, meant there was some incentive to utilise the expenses system, shall we say. I was never a major fiddler. History demands an honest account, though. Advised by more experienced hands, one would take the green single decker bus from the stop right outside the head office, and spend about a shilling on the fare to South Merstham. Subbed copy safely delivered, there was no great urgency about returning. I have always enjoyed walking anyway. Each trip would therefore mean a shilling spent, and two shillings claimed.

Another non-writing job involved getting a reporter's work from a district office at Oxted to be subbed in the shed at Redhill. One Jack Bone was the district man in Oxted. Once he'd written his copy, he would hand it to the conductor of a bus – yes, most buses once had conductors as well as drivers – who would hand it over to a head office junior upon arrival in Redhill. Bone would call up, and traffic being

40

reasonably light then, you could time your stroll to the stop and know the bus would be just arriving. More confessions now. When I had become too senior to wander around collecting and delivering copy, I was among those who would inform the youngest reporter present that the Oxted copy was on the next bus, even when it wasn't. We would always wait till it was raining hard to indulge in this prank, and get our pleasure from the worried face of the junior when he returned, soaking, and apologising for somehow missing the precious parcel. What rats we were.

No task bored me. I enjoyed getting and writing up every story. It could be anything, from the routines of court and council reporting, to house fires, crimes, and then all the other 'nice' news that so many hacks seem to despise. A local fête, or a garden show? Hard to make interesting – but that was the challenge. There was once a strike by telephone operators, then employed by the General Post Office. Almost all phone calling these days is automatic: operators play little part. In the 1960s they were still important, especially for long distance or foreign calls. It must have been a fairly gentlemanly example of 'industrial action' – one of those casual phrases meaning the exact opposite – as it started at 10.30 one evening.

How to make the story live a bit? I decided to go back to the office just before half past ten, and on the stroke of 10.30, I sat at the *Surrey Mirror* switchboard, pushed a plug into place, and got through to a GPO operator. I requested a long distance number, and was politely told there was no question of being connected. 'Just after 10.30, our reporter tried . . .' ran the story.

Life was reasonably peaceful, or perhaps we did not 'flam up' minor crime stories in quite the way many papers, local and national, do now. We did have several murders, but the most dramatic incident was an armed siege in a place with the wholly inappropriate name of Tranquil Dale, in a little place called Betchworth. I still pass it almost every day, and always think back to a dramatic few night-time hours in a young reporter's life. Some domestic argument had turned violent in what had until then been a quiet stub of a cul-de-sac. Nowadays, the police would undoubtedly keep everyone, Press and all, well back. Things were a good deal less excitable in Betchworth circa 1966. I parked my car – more on my various rickety vehicles later – a hundred yards or so away, and strolled along Tranquil Dale.

A policeman was crouching beside his car. 'I wouldn't wander about if I were you,' he said. 'The bloke's got a rifle.' Sure enough, there he was, waving the gun out of an upstairs window. The patience of the police eventually ran out, a small quantity of tear gas was used, and our gunman was marched out and off to the nearest nick. It was about the first story that attracted those near-mythical beasts, the Fleet Street papers. In the darkness, a smart car drew up, and a photographer got out. He set up his camera, a couple of flashes went off, and he strode off, announcing: 'That picture will be on the front page of tomorrow's *Daily Express*.' And so it was.

What was absent was any sign of a *television* camera, or indeed a radio microphone. Newspapers ruled the roost. My page one piece ended with something on the lines of 'Tranquil Dale went back to living up to its name once more.' I have always thought I could have found a more elegant way to express the thought. But it was a very good story.

Another good story, if a sad one, came at a time when the vagaries of the *Surrey Mirror*'s staffing meant I was asked to stand in for the Sports Editor for a while. The regular Sports Editor was a dreadfully thin man with a racking cough not improved by heavy smoking. He may have written copiously about sports; I thought it most unlikely he could have taken part in any of them. I was not a great choice to replace him – not that there was much choice – because sport has never held enormous interest for me. I had enjoyed my cricket at school, never my football. And it was the football season. Still, it was a challenge. I had sole charge of several pages, and had to write many of the stories, and sub edit all of them.

One Saturday found me covering the amateur football in Redhill's Memorial Park. The stand faced east, and as so often during the winter there was a chill wind blowing straight in from somewhere in the Siberia area. I concentrated feverishly on which 'Red' had the ball at every moment, in case he suddenly turned out to be a goal scorer. Alongside me in the Press box was a reporter for the paper covering the district where the opposing team was based. Barnet in North London, I think it was.

The game was pretty lifeless, until it was interrupted abruptly by a loud explosion and a pall of smoke going up behind a row of houses on the other side of the ground. A few seconds' thought led me to the only conclusion. I had to find out what the blast was all about. Don't worry, said the Barnet reporter. He promised to keep an eye on the game and tell me later what happened. Round the back of the row of houses there had been a desperate accident. A couple of boys had been mucking around with fireworks. One was thrown into a tank containing a dangerous liquid called Toluene, and the explosion seriously injured the youngsters. I got there about the same time as the fire and the ambulance people. Manhole covers were hopping into the air as the blazing liquid coursed into the drains.

Over the next few days I followed the story, as horribly worried relatives trooped back and forth to the local hospital where the boys had been taken. At some stage, I called the guy from Barnet to check on the football match. In my absence the Reds had won, having scored several times. He gave me the names. Some names anyway.

At the end of the week, I had the satisfaction of having the main stories on both the front and back pages: the explosion, and the Redhill team's victory. It was not a complete journalistic triumph, however. The Deputy Editor, a wintry soul called Goddard, unlike the genial Editor Cecil Gegg, praised me for my resourceful coverage of the firework incident. He had to advise me in grave tones that the names of the local goal scorers in my sports report were all wrong. I have often wondered whether Barnet deliberately misled Redhill that Saturday afternoon.

I had come from schooldays fairly innocent in the world's wicked ways. Reporting the local magistrates' court often opened my eyes. One smooth barrister down from London grew tired of a thick young man's answers in a sex offence case. He had tried a string of questions. Had the man slept with the girl? Had he been intimate with her? Various other polite expressions were tried. The defendant failed over and over again to get the drift of the interrogation. Finally, exasperation won out. 'We are all men of the world here,' declaimed the barrister. 'Did you *fuck* her?' The young man brightened up: 'Oh yeah . . . I *fucked* her . . .'

Even more shocking for the young reporter on the Press bench who probably blushed very easily was to sit and listen while the prosecution in another case announced that a grubby-looking man in the dock had been charged with 'offences involving chickens'. There were some very rural backwaters in Surrey in those days. Sometimes violence erupted in the courtroom itself. A Redhill family had a reputation for breeding thugs. One was up on a charge, and when the verdict to send him off to prison came in, he leapt from the dock, and lashed out at the coppers who tried to stop him running away.

The grimmest legal moments came with coroners' inquests. This quaint old institution is a strange way of establishing causes of death, which are very often blindingly obvious from the start. It was not easy

43

being in the same room as relatives and friends listened to the tragic way someone's life had ended. One man killed himself after I had written about his appearance in court on some charge of dishonesty. He had pleaded with me to keep it out of the paper. I knew what to say. He would have to take it up with my Editor. Whether he did or not, the piece went in. Straightforward journalism can have miserable consequences.

On other occasions I had dramas of my own involving the police and the court. When I joined the *Surrey Mirror*, I had yet to pass my driving test. At the third attempt, I made it, in my Dad's car, a Ford Consul 375. It wallowed around like a boat, and I nearly turned it over a few days after the successful test. My father must have been relieved by my anxiety to get my own car. He took me to a car dealer in the back streets of Hackbridge, where a salesman with a small moustache and a tired-looking raincoat agreed to sell me a Ford Anglia, made in 1949, for £45. I drove Dad round the block to test it out, misjudged a corner, clipped a lorry, and came back to the dealer with a wing hanging half off. He knocked the price down to £35, and the wing flapped around ever afterwards. And the rain got in, and smoke poured through the floorboards when accelerating, and . . . let's just say the Anglia had many foibles.

I finally got rid of the Anglia, and got a smarter and more up to date Ford Prefect. Even though my pay had risen from the £7.25 a week I started on, getting somewhere short of £10 meant that finding the cash for petrol, oil, insurance *and* car tax could be a strain. During one lean period, I was driving round with an out of date tax disc in the front windscreen. After court finished one day, I got into the untaxed Prefect to drive the couple of miles back to the office. The inspector from the police station close to the paper's headquarters, who had been in court, came across the car park, leant in – and asked for a lift back. For two sweat-laden miles I drove along gingerly, aware that right in front of the officer was the evidence of a road traffic offence. He must have noticed. He said nothing.

The same car developed an annoying habit of not starting in the morning. In spite of my modest pay packet, I had moved into a bedsit, managing to find the £3 a week rent. It was in a tall house at the top of a steep hill. Steep enough to allow me most days to roll my car down the hill, and 'bump' start it before the bottom. For younger generations for whom that might sound like something rude, it involved engaging a middling gear, and letting the clutch out once speed picked up. Usually this did the trick, and the engine would cough into life. One morning, no joy. I left the car on a tricky bend at the foot of the hill. I returned a few hours later to find a parking ticket wedged under a wiper blade. I took it to the police station, where I knew the desk sergeant well: I would chat to him most days in the quest for stories. He looked at the ticket and tutted. 'Here, give me that.' He tore it in half, and chucked it in a bin behind him. Happy, far off days.

That car was fated in other ways. There was the time I stopped on a hilly road to get directions from the crew of a refuse lorry parked on the other side. I walked over to them, asked where a particular street was, and got the answer: 'Before I tell you that ... your car's running away.' So it was. Gently it made off downhill and rolled into a lamp post. I don't think I ever bothered to get the dent in the front bumper straightened out. Or have the faulty handbrake adjusted.

There were extremely enjoyable assignments. I was always fascinated to interview centenarians. Most of the 100-year-olds were women, naturally. Was there one clue to a very long life? I decided there was not. Some, of either sex, had never touched alcohol. Some had always enjoyed a tipple. Some had worked very hard, some had enjoyed a sheltered and uneventful existence. All reckoned they had the secret of outliving everyone else. Members of the local branch of the 'Old Contemptibles' were not quite 100 years old, but their numbers had dwindled to the point where the local branch was closing down. I went to the final meeting. It was a last chance to hear stories told by men who had been among the first to march away to war in 1914. They took their name proudly from what the Kaiser had said of them: 'A contemptible little army.' Strange for my generation to realise that now, few survive who were in at the start of the *Second* World War.

Cecil Gegg was not my only mentor. Another man who had considerable influence was an ex *Daily Mirror* sub editor who I think must have been sacked by them for any number of personal reasons. He had been forced to 'trade down' to the demeaning job of being chief sub for the *Surrey Mirror*. He brought some of his bruising Fleet Street ways with him. He would reject pieces written by reporters by scrunching up and hurling their work back at them. All this accompanied by yelling and vigorous language. I learned fast that he would be pleased when a little thought and effort transformed a drearily-done story into an interesting one. The golden rule was that the first paragraph, the 'intro', should grab the reader's attention, creating interest. You might say, create excitement. As has been observed now and then, writing a piece for a newspaper is one of the few activities where the orgasm comes at the beginning.

Outsiders often marvel at how little training someone like me has received. There was, back half a century ago, a day release scheme for journalists which involved a weekly trip to a technical college in Guildford to be told about layout, newspaper law, and various other basic aspects of the craft. I was always hoping to find an excuse not to go. A perfect one came one day. Gas mains in the centre of Redhill exploded. I was the only reporter around. I dismissed myself from the Tech course, and got to work on a jolly good story. When the day release courses ended, I sat exams with as much trepidation as my doomed Physics and French 'O' levels. Yet I received a high overall mark. I was one of two Owens on the course. I have often wondered whether there was a mix-up between candidates. If there was ... Michael Owen, who was to spend years writing about arts on the London *Evening Standard* ... please accept my apologies.

Shorthand was supposed to be grasped. I never could. I tried evening classes at a local night school. All the other students were would-be secretary girls. It was either distraction or lack of concentration that scuppered me there. I tried a teacher in the town who was a real expert. He lived in a tall, gloomy house, and after a several knocks, it took an age for an ancient man to open the creaking front door. He could have been a servant in one of Dracula's residences. It turned out that he had learned shorthand from Sir Isaac Pitman himself, in the 1890s. I still never mastered the great man's invention.

I did learn how to sub edit copy, and how to lay out pages. During my sports editing I was in total charge of everything from gathering the stories, editing them, and getting the pages sorted out. One week I arrived at the print setters to find great gaps at the bottom of the metal type. 'You haven't written enough,' a friendly compositor pointed out. Having miscalculated how much type would fill the sports section, I had to set to hastily and write some extra, and large, headlines, to bulk out the pages. Later on, being able to 'cast off' accurately, and read set type backwards, would come in handy in a much grander print shop.

Sometimes, especially in the summer, news was short. I was responsible for ferreting out tales from the village of Merstham. I hit upon the idea of a summertime series profiling local worthies. People like the

Roman Catholic priest. That got the paper, and me, into hot water. The *Surrey Mirror*'s style was to give all clergymen their full title when first referred to. So it would be 'Rev John Smith' at first. Subsequent references would be to 'Mr Smith'. Following my paper's style, the priest became 'Mr' after a few sentences. His flock, like all Catholics, called him 'Father'. He was furious, and did not speak to me again.

EIGHT

Gathering local news was my idea of heaven. Well, almost. My eyes became fixed increasingly on getting to Fleet Street, then still very much the heart of the newspaper business. We had occasional visits from London reporters: they were always sharp fellows in fast cars. There was a *Daily Sketch* man who pursued the story of oil being discovered in mid-Surrey. His research quite clearly centred on the saloon bars of various country pubs. Another time I shared a helicopter with an *Evening Standard* reporter as we were invited to survey how little damage had been done to the countryside by a large network of new gas pipes that had been laid. I admired his quickly thought-up description of a 'spider's web' of pipes . . . and plagiarised it for the local paper.

My part of Surrey was changing and developing rapidly. The M23 and M25 motorways were to carve through my area, bringing the roar of traffic to what had been quiet woods and valleys, and smothering part of the route of what could claim to be the world's first public rail route. Opened in the early 1800s, the Surrey Iron Railway was horse-drawn to get stone from quarries in the county to the Thames at Wandsworth. One day I gazed down into a hole on one of the motorway construction sites to see some original, primitive rails which had been uncovered. When I went to look at the motorway plans, I discovered that the intersection between the two of them would sprawl over 153 acres, obliterating at least one small hamlet in the process. I drove round to have a look at the quiet little community that would be buried when the road builders arrived.

Sometimes a local reporter had a story good enough to sell to the national Press. Getting involved with Fleet Street was a two-way process. Editors in London wanted stories, and they would often need help to follow up the local angle of a national news item. A network of local correspondents was relied on. Round our way, it was the *Surrey Mirror*'s chief reporter, one Monty Burton. He was 'Burton of Redhill' to the busy news desks in London. Burton gave in his notice after taking a job with a trade magazine. At his leaving drink-up in a pub close to the office I asked him who would succeed him as the 'stringer' for the nationals. 'You can do it if you want,' he said. I certainly did want. 'Owen of Redhill' became the one agitating to get pieces into the dailies, and grateful for the extra few pounds they paid.

The title was of great help when it came to knocking on Fleet Street doors. People knew vaguely who I was. I had several discussions with intimidating news editors of papers like the *Daily Mirror*, then the biggest weekday beast in Fleet Street. Although Percy Trumble did not actually wear an eye shade, he looked and sounded every inch like a gritty newspaper executive in a black and white film. His first move was to dangle the letter I'd written to him, and invite me to spot the silly spelling mistake in it. He then had a suggestion. I should take myself up North and get experience of daily journalism in one of the hard-bitten places where boys became newspaper men. Strangely, I would follow that advice a decade or so later. In 1968, however, I did not fancy such a pilgrimage. For one important thing, I was about to get married. So it was that a much more attractive post was offered and accepted on the *Evening Standard*.

I will never forget the sad but resigned look on the face of my revered *Surrey Mirror* editor Cecil Gegg when I told him I was off. And there was the astonishment of colleagues when I brandished a letter from the *Standard* confirming my pay at £20 a week. In fact, shortly after I started, someone spotted that I was getting less than the agreed minimum, and my salary leapt to £30 a week.

I joined the City Office of the *Standard*. My father was still a faithful servant of the merchant bank Rothschilds, so I knew my way roughly round the Square Mile. So many journalists profess to be innumerate, almost as a badge of honour. In spite of giving up maths even before sitting my O levels, I was mentally nimble enough with figures. Even so, the interview with the City Editor, Robin Purdue, was daunting. Partly because I had no idea what he meant when he told me they were busy because the pound was 'roaring its head off' – it was under extreme pressure in the foreign exchanges – and also because my one decent suit had a small but embarrassing hole in the seat of the trousers. When I was not sitting down I held my hands carefully together behind me like a patrolling policeman. Purdue did not seem to notice, and took me on.

Financial reporting has been centre stage in recent times, thanks to the calamities of the recent worldwide crises. It was more of a backwater in the late 1960s, in spite of events like the devaluation of sterling and the beginnings of the huge economic changes in Britain as old industries declined. Still, it was Fleet Street, with all its terrors and excitements.

Within days of joining, my personal journalistic world was thrown upside down. I had groped my way through my first week of trying desperately to learn not only how a renowned evening paper worked, but also how the City functioned. The following Monday would be shattering. I arrived at the City office in Moorgate to be told abruptly by another reporter to go out and have breakfast. My protest that I had already eaten was waved away. Just get out. It emerged that Robin Purdue, the young City Editor who had hired me, who had talked of the roaring pound, had committed suicide over the weekend. I never did learn the full extent of the domestic and perhaps financial miseries that made him do it. His body had been discovered by his deputy, Jack Prosser.

After that trauma, I settled into the routine of a very busy office. The *Standard* was fighting hard against the *Evening News*. There were several editions a day, and woe betide you if you were beaten on a story by the *News*. Our Editor was the fiercesome Charles Wintour, a gifted yet irascible man, father of Anna Wintour, who would in her turn go to New York and edit *Vogue*. Her brisk ways have sometimes earned the unkind nickname 'Nuclear' Wintour. The same could have applied to her dad.

TV and the Internet have eaten away at the old battling ways of newspapers. The *Standard* even became a 'giveaway' in 2009. We lived and died by tight deadlines and intense competition, and it was a thrilling ride for a lad from the Surrey sticks. By-lines were few and far between, as on the *Surrey Mirror*. My heart raced the day I got a 'By Nick Owen' on the front page of the *Standard*'s last edition. It was too late to be seen by more than a few readers but I gloried in the recognition. Our final deadline for the 'fudge' – the box on the front page where late news was carried in blurry type – was 5.25 to get stuff into that evening's last edition.

A marvellous bunch of characters shared our office, amid the clatter of typewriters and the chatter of news agency telexes. Jack Prosser became an urbane City Editor after the unfortunate Purdue. His deputy was an immensely likeable and cheery man called Hugh Sharpe who several times a day would hammer out hundreds of words on an old typewriter in a few noisy minutes. Among the City reporters was Doreen Chaundy, who earlier in life had been a secretary to some of the great editors in the Express group. Jim Levi, a superb financial journalist, became a lifelong friend.

John Jones was a big Cockney lad, always immaculately dressed, who had a sharp nose for news. Most hectic days, he would write and then rewrite for successive editions the stock market reports, charting the rise and fall of leading shares. In that he was assisted by Bill Gee. Bill was a veteran of City offices, a lovely, tubby man getting on in years who would be in before everyone else, and who would always head out early for a decent lunch with informative chums. His job was to find out what was happening to share prices, and why. Lunchtime over, trouble would often come when an impatient John Jones would try to get information out of Bill. 'Why are prices up, Billy?' Jones would ask. Gee would draw on his cigarette, peer round, and declare: 'More buyers than sellers.' True, but hardly helpful in explaining what was going on. An irritated Jones would bat the well-lunched Bill Gee around the head with a rolled-up newspaper.

We had to cover every sort of financial story, from changing mortgage rates – young journalists tend to write a lot about them, because they are so often over-borrowed on their own homes – to boardroom battles and companies either trumpeting their successes or struggling to stay afloat. I got a decent front page piece, with a rare front page by-line, for some rather doubtful guff about a revolutionary new car engine. We would all have to wait till the next century for anything practical on those lines. A major task from mid-afternoons onwards was to find 'overnights', pieces that could be written before going home, to fill the early editions the next day. It was a great test of journalistic ingenuity, ferreting out interesting tales that, if good enough, could last through every edition.

One particularly interesting day found me at the Great Eastern Hotel beside Liverpool Street station, attending a Press conference at which a hawk-eyed young Australian newspaper proprietor talked of his plans to buy that long-established Fleet Street rag the *News of the World*. The Aussie was Rupert Murdoch. Later he would acquire the new but ailing *Sun* for a few quid, turning it into a cheeky tabloid with unclad girls on page three. Many years later I was told by one of his lieutenants that Murdoch, offered for the first issue under his management a picture of a girl with both bits of her bikini on, or one with only the bottom section, himself picked the topless shot. Rupert Murdoch was beginning to build the worldwide empire that would eventually lurch into the crises that dominated all newspaper headlines in the summer of 2011, the *News of the World* itself being shut down.

We *Evening Standard* staff shared a first floor office in Moorgate, a few hundred yards north of the Bank of England, with the City departments of the *Daily Express* and the *Sunday Express*. The *Sunday* team made few appearances until the end of the week, having grandly wined and dined their way around their contacts to get what they hoped would be scoops – exclusives – for the weekend. The *Daily* staff were not around much in the mornings, then burst into action mid-afternoon. The City Editor was a tall, thin man who had served the press baron Lord Beaverbrook for many years. Fred Ellis was one of the diminishing band of City men who wore a bowler. He had a blazing temper: at least one typewriter was hurled out of his office as he bellowed at a journalist for some shortcoming or other. One anger-filled afternoon, he demanded to know what one of his reporters, absent for what had obviously been a very long and very liquid lunch, had actually been doing. 'I've been gathering and a-garnering, sir ... gathering and a-garnering,' replied the underling, swaying slightly as he did so.

Booze ruled, and expenses were plentiful. An old journalist friend of mine came from Birmingham to work for the *Daily Express*. After his first week or two, he put in quite a big expenses claim. He was called in to see a boss, who made it clear the amount was quite unacceptable. It had to be even larger, otherwise queries might be raised about other reporters' claims. Days and attitudes that are long, long gone.

Another title that was just about managing to survive was the *Daily Sketch*. Most days it was a pallid imitation of the then still mighty *Daily Mirror*. To do some reporting for it would, however, be a way of getting morning paper experience, and I managed to talk my way into getting shifts at the *Sketch*. After a hard day in Jack Prosser's *Evening Standard* office I was a *Sketch* 'casual' by night, when most sensible people had gone home. Often I would not finish before three in the morning. They were the sort of fascinating hours that Grandad Frisby worked.

Heaven knows where I got the energy from. The *Daily Sketch* newsroom was on the first floor of a grimy building down a lane just a few yards south of Fleet Street itself. Everything around resonated with the exciting business of turning out newspapers. Before the presses started thundering away, lorries would arrive with a giant rolls of newsprint – why 'print' when it was still plain paper is a nice little oddity – which had to be lowered gingerly off the back of the trucks. When the rolls thumped down, the whole roadway would shake.

Trouble was, the *Sketch* was finished and everyone in Fleet Street knew it. The *Mirror*, and the slipping but then still powerful *Daily Express*, were throttling this poor relation in the Associated Newspapers stable. Dying it may have been, but the *Sketch* had some canny people running it. David English was the Editor. The news editor, my immediate and much-feared boss, was one Brian Walmsley. The parlous state of the *Sketch* created much paranoia around the newsroom. Walmsley was convinced that any good story the paper stumbled on would be passed on for a small fee to one of its rivals by some traitor in the ranks. So if there was a juicy idea around, Walmsley would send trusted reporters out and tell them to call in from a convenient telephone box. Mobiles, if you ever encountered any, were still cumbersome and very *im*mobile.

I followed Walmsley's usual orders one evening and found a phone box near Blackfriars Bridge to call him. The whispered order was to go immediately to Southend. The rumour was that a couple of women had actually gone through some sort of wedding ceremony. This was the 1960s, swinging in some ways but desperately prudish in others. A scandal was scented. Off I rattled in my latest unreliable car. I remember nearly turning it over on the Commercial Road as I sped eastwards.

Somehow I discovered where the two women lived. They let me in, and a cautious waltzing around the sensitive information began. I tried not to be too distracted by a baby, someone's baby, who was asleep in the corner of their small and dingy flat. The women explained that much as they would like to help me, they had sold their story to a Sunday paper. I would never have been that good at being a tabloid reporter – one of my daughters would eventually be a very gifted one – although on this occasion I did manage to prise out the story.

I told the couple that I quite understood their prior arrangement. I would, however, have to explain to my news desk why I had failed to get any copy. And the only way to do that would be to have all the facts. Amazingly, they told me them. The *Sketch* had its story. As a result it is most unlikely the Sunday paper paid up. I may have had a twinge of conscience. I would never have managed such a dodgy trick if they had had access to a wily adviser like Max Clifford.

Pundits today, marvelling at the rise of bloggers and the like, ask sometimes what is the point of papers, even of TV and radio, in this information-soaked age. What is undeniable is that newspapers have changed radically. And will have to change a lot more. No change is as painful as a paper that has to close. The *Daily Sketch* was a paper that died, and I saw what happened as it succumbed. The *Sketch* was being hammered in the circulation war between the *Daily Mirror* and the *Daily Express*. We were very short of money and staff. The other national dailies had big guns to our puny pistols. For instance, the *Express* had the legendary Chapman Pincher, a defence correspondent who churned out scoops almost every night. The *Mirror* had some of the best journalistic writers ever born. Often a hapless *Sketch* reporter who thought he or she had finished for the day would be rung at home by an irate Brian Walmsley and told to follow up a headline in one of the other tabloids. At the *Sketch*, those rats who could get off the sinking ship were busy doing so.

A few loyalists still hunted for exclusives to attract readers and try to hold on to advertisers. One evening, I was the only one in the newsroom available to report on the Prince of Wales visiting a theatre, in the company of a young woman. This was years before the appearance of a pretty, shy girl called Diana Spencer. The Prince was due to go with someone the newspapers of the day liked to refer to as 'a mystery woman'. Nowadays with Google, Twitter, Facebook and goodness knows what else, we would almost certainly have known who she was before the curtain went up. In those days, she was just a very young unknown. Naturally, she was from a 'good family', as they used to say. Otherwise, she was a mystery indeed to us hacks.

I arrived to find the play had already started, and I was ushered into the manager's office to await the end of the performance and the opportunity to see Prince Charles leave. Battalions of my colleagues from rival papers were there well ahead of me in the manager's den. The poor old *Sketch* tended to be the last to find out what was going on. The noise of applause at the final curtain call was the signal to scramble outside.

We waited on the pavement for the Prince to appear. Charles was one of the world's most eligible bachelors and pictures of him in the paper with his mysterious friend were guaranteed to push up sales, so flash bulbs went off like a lightning storm as the couple appeared. I had been elbowed to the end of the line, which meant I was nearest to the Prince's escape – his limousine. As the Prince walked towards his car, guiding his companion past Fleet Street's finest, I was in his way. My colleagues and Charles's detectives stared at me. Who was this upstart, daring to delay the Prince on his night out? Gulping away the nerves, I posed my penetrating question:

'Did . . . did you enjoy the play, Sir?'

Prince Charles glanced at me. In years to come, when we would encounter each other in all sorts of unlikely places the length and breadth of the Earth, there would usually be a Princely glare of irritation if I emerged from the media pack to try to ask something. In 1969, both of us barely out of our teens, he smiled a bit thinly . . . and said: 'Yes, thank you, very much,' and tried to get to his car. As he manoeuvred past me, he stepped firmly on to my foot. He and his lady friend finally clambered into the limousine, which swept away to another burst of photographers' flashbulbs.

An aching foot. Scowling bodyguards. Irritated competitors. No matter. I had my scoop, and what a wonderful one it was, too. No-one else had managed to speak to His Royal Highness, so I was able to send the story through with a magical ingredient for the all-important and compelling 'intro'. It ran:

'The Prince of Wales told the *Daily* Sketch last night . . .'

I was not long at the *Sketch*. It was fading away. Those working for its stable mate the *Daily Mail* assumed they would be nice and safe and the *Daily Sketch* staff would all be out of a job. Wrong. The *Sketch* died, but Editor David English and news editor Brian Walmsley were switched to the *Mail*, where they played their all-important parts in making it the most clued-up, if not always the most temperate, of the national newspapers.

NINE

In the midst of all the City reporting and the helter-skelter chasing after late-night stories for the *Sketch*, I got married. In 1968, Philippa Bigg, whose father ran a filling station and garage in a village a few miles from Kingswood, became Mrs Owen. The next year, our daughter Rebecca was born. It was time to think about what sort of journalist this family man really wanted to be. I decided that I did not fancy a tabloid hack's life. I also wanted to move on from an evening paper. I contacted the City Office of the *Daily Telegraph* and asked for a job. Another interesting character shaped the next stage of my journalistic journey. It is often said that the old Fleet Street was full of characters. I certainly met a few. Kenneth Fleet was one of them. He was a terrific City Editor of the *Telegraph*. He always wanted to rise to be Editor of the paper, a job he never managed to slog his way up to.

I once heard the legendary – an overused adjective but not in this case – Hugh Cudlipp, who had been the greatest of *Daily Mirror* Editors, describe what becoming a national paper editor was like. Rising through the journalistic ranks, he said, was like climbing a mountain. You start down in the lush valley, where life is easy. It's very pleasant when you go up through the foothills. Though the country is still reasonably gentle, the walk gradually becomes that bit stiffer. Onward, and the climb gets much harder, the weather worse. As you near the storm-lashed summit, other poor wretches come staggering back the other way, bawling: 'Don't go … don't go any further!' You do. It's a terrible struggle. You are shattered in mind, body, and spirit. When you get to the top, however, the view is absolutely amazing. You are consumed by an incredible feeling of triumph. Only one way to go afterwards, of course …

Ken Fleet never made the Editor's chair, only the one in the City Office. Fleet was a striking individual. He was quite short, with a large head and a bearing that was almost Roman. His jet black hair was waved back a tad, and there always seemed to be a slight smile playing around his lips. He liked sports cars – a trait he shared with another City Editor who lay in my future – and attractive women. Together, if possible. The smile often gave way to a chuckle, especially if a good story had been sniffed out. Or sometimes if a powerful figure had been discomfited by some revelation. One afternoon, he grinned broadly as some legal functionary marched in, and handed him a writ for libel.

For myself, it wasn't so much working with Fleet that appealed. Wanting to be on a morning national, the *Daily Telegraph* had been my first choice. After all, it had been delivered at home. And when he got back from the City, my Dad would always bring the *Evening Standard*, on which I had also worked. How neat to be employed by the two titles that were family favourites. I wrote to Fleet, he interviewed me, and I awaited his verdict. A letter arrived, with dread words on the lines of 'Thank you for coming to see me. I regret . . .' Then some stuff about no vacancies at present, keeping your name on file, and so forth. In other words: forget it, lad.

The very next day, another letter from Fleet. Rather different. 'Thank you for coming to see me. I am pleased to be able to offer you . . .' I decided quickly to ignore letter number one and proceed on the basis of number two. Recalling the Guildford exam mix-up, I have often wondered whether the second one was intended for someone else. Perhaps there was simply a last-minute need to find a new reporter. Whatever had happened, it was great for me.

The farcical appointment process was followed by a barmy start to my full-time days at a morning paper. Neither Fleet nor I had noticed that my agreed first day was a Bank Holiday Monday. The *Telegraph* City Office was on the top floor at the back of what was then the *Financial Times*'s aptly darkish pink, unlovely HQ, Bracken House, close to St Paul's Cathedral. On a Bank Holiday, a very quiet part of London. It was very quiet in the *Telegraph* office too. Only myself and one other writer, bemused by my presence, came in. He reassured me that, one way and another, with almost everyone including Kenneth Fleet having a day off, I should skedaddle.

Once the Bank Holiday was over, I began to get used to a different rhythm of work. It was a great change of pace from the *Evening Standard*. The *Standard*'s City Office had been a frenetic place, from well before 9 a.m. until after 6 at night. Phones jangling, typewriters being bashed, and constant banter between hard-pressed writers always having an eye to another deadline zooming up. At the *Telegraph*, mornings were a light canter. The news editor, who marshalled the reporting troops and allocated their duties – the tall cigar-chomping John Davies – would stride in with a few other senior figures to have a meeting with Fleet. What would we be covering? Fleet was mostly concerned about his own column, which ran across the top of the first City page. He was content to leave most other coverage to Davies and his staff.

Not many of us would put finger to typewriter before the afternoon. There was one important exception. Roland – always 'Roly' – Gribben, the Business Editor, was never idle. He turned out story after story throughout the day. Throughout the years too. He became a firm friend, and in his 70s, still worked part-time for the *Daily Telegraph*, his by-line frequently topping several different pieces in the financial pages. I have always admired this master of the craft who began his career on the *Hexham Courant* in Northumberland. We have discussed endlessly the ups and downs of our trade as we tramp round golf courses, two people for whom journalism has never lost its magic.

As the morning rolled by, plans would be laid for lunch. Not always for personal pleasure only. In the 1970s, a lot of City stories, intentionally or sometimes unintentionally, would be disclosed over a few glasses of wine and a solid meal. It was a bad week if at least once I did not end up at one of the big London hotels, where as well as lunches, Press conferences were often held. In the afternoons the tempo picked up. I began to corner the market in big, later breaking stories. It was always fun to be hurrying to get a piece finished before the early evening deadline.

It was the era of big takeovers. Household names like Trumans, the famous brewers, were battled over and shareholders bombarded with claims and counter claims from the rival boards of directors. Often the stories were big enough to make the front page. On one occasion, a sub editor down the road in Peterborough Court, the Fleet Street headquarters of the *Telegraph* empire, got my name slightly wrong. My by-line one morning was 'Nicholson Owen'. Sounded quite good. I did wonder whether to stick with it.

It was, however, with a proper 'By Nicholas Owen' that my big moment came. Vehicle and General was a motor insurance company that went bust. It happened suddenly. The drama was of the highest. Motorists' insurance policies became invalid at once. The piece, leading the paper's front page, highlighted the advice that drivers must not get behind the wheel until they had made new arrangements. The *Telegraph* switchboard was, as they say, jammed. The collapse of V and G led to important reforms in motor insurance cover. A guarantee scheme was set up so that car owners would not again find themselves stranded without insurance.

The morning it all broke, I happened to go to see a friend of mine, not a journalist, who had an office just off Fleet Street itself. I could not have felt more excited. I always tell young journalists that nothing can ever beat your by-line on the front page of a newspaper. Television reporting, or even presenting, never brings quite that satisfaction. As I sat down in my friend's office, there, cast to the floor, was the latest *Daily Telegraph*. *My* name was on the biggest story on page one. He never mentioned it. I didn't feel I should. Like many readers, he no doubt scanned the first few paragraphs, and failed to register who had written what.

The routine of big stories late in the day left me time to think about other parts of journalism. I have always been wary of mixing outside interests with the day job. Now and again, I have made exceptions. In 1972, the famous Brighton Belle train was taken out of service. I offered to write about it for the *Telegraph*'s Magazine. The Belle was the sort of train that doesn't exist any more. It only took just under an hour to get between the coast and London, but had a lot of show business names among its regular clientele. The cast list would often include Laurence Olivier and Dora Bryan, Brighton residents who would often be learning lines as they ate their breakfast kippers, served by Pullman staff who combined the wearing of white jackets with perfect manners. The Belle was romantic railwaying, and it made a super feature for the magazine.

I am a railway enthusiast, that often derided species. I have always worn my anorak with pride, though I draw the line at thermos flasks and a grubby bag of unedifying sandwiches. And I do not jot down train numbers either. Still, an enthusiast is what I am, and unashamedly. One particular meeting of enthusiasts, a real anoraks' get-together, again in 1972, embraced other faiths. One group declared themselves *trolleybus* fans. Trolleys – some sensible cities abroad still have them – draw electric power from overhead wires but run on ordinary tyres. A mix of tram and bus, and surely an environmentally desirable method of urban transport. Sadly, demand for diesel buses was such that UK manufacturers preferred to build those, and while everyone was still sure oil would always be cheap, trolley building got squeezed out. Were any still running, I wondered? Yes, I was told, the last system was in Bradford – where curiously, the first trolleybuses had appeared, in 1909 – though it was due to close in a few weeks. A story, I thought.

I went to Bradford, chatted with trolleybus crews and passengers, and wrote a feature for the *Telegraph*'s news pages. There was a surprising sequel. A few days later a letter arrived from the publishers David and Charles. They had been looking for someone to do a history of the trolleybus. They thought I was just the man to write the definitive work. It was the sort of slightly offbeat challenge that I have always found hard to resist. For nine months there was much enjoyable flitting about the country, digging through old local council files, and chatting to blokes, some very elderly and long retired, who had driven the trolleybuses, directed their operations, or even in one case designed the wiring once draped around lots of towns and cities like cats' cradles some twenty or so feet in the air.

When the book came out I tried to ignore at least one howling error that no-one has ever been impolite enough to point out. I was amazed to get a decent royalty cheque after a year. Anyone who was interested, even if there were not that many of them, bought a copy. Nowadays, transport nuts write about every conceivable bit of bus or railway operation. In its day, *The History of the British Trolleybus* was one of very few books on the subject. If you think trolleybus fans must be about as rare as children who go happily to bed early, I must tell you that quite a few people over the three and half decades since publication have thrust their copy at me and asked for a signature.

Having time to write a book showed that working life on the *Telegraph* was not too arduous. Because I usually did the bigger stories, they often got on to the front page. As well as the Vehicle and General collapse, there were huge takeovers going on, as companies like BP began in the early 1970s to expand into and even dominate world markets. A couple of times, I got myself over to Northern Ireland, then in the early grip of the 'Troubles'. There were business stories to do as the province became a war zone where civilians, soldiers and police officers were being killed almost every day. There was always something surreal in walking down roads that looked like any other part of Britain – from the names on some of the shops to the very street signs themselves – while the paraphernalia of urban conflict was on every side.

I remember being close by when Irish republicans fired from a tower block in Belfast. An armoured car swept up, and a classic young British

NCO stuck his head out of the top and in a public school accent drawled out a question to anyone who would listen: 'Does anyone know where that shooting's coming from?' Sometimes you could see why the British could be strongly disliked by those they ruled over. One evening there was the nasty thump of a bomb going off, and the sound of the glass in my hotel window coming in, just as I was phoning home to say I was fine and safe. Another night I drove to the hills on the outskirts of Belfast, got out of the car, and listened to the distinctive, if distant, patter-patter of a machine gun.

It was strange to drive a few miles south, into the tranquil countryside of the Irish Republic. Dublin was of course at peace, though it was a poor city in the 1970s, smelling of coal smoke, with many beggars on the streets. In the 1990s, piles of European money transformed the Irish economy, property prices rocketed, and few people looked short of money. Begging became more of a common sight in London. Nemesis was to come to Ireland in the 21st century, as financial bubbles burst and whole countries staggered towards ruin.

The *Telegraph* I knew was still owned by Lord Hartwell's family and had a reputation for not being a great breaker of news, especially of anything that might upset the Conservative party. All very different from the *Telegraph* that would have such an impact when it did a devastatingly good job of exposing MPs' expenses in 2009. The main office used to be in the heart of Fleet Street. And a pretty inefficient outfit it was too. It was well established that a journalist short of cash only had to wander into Peterborough Court, under a famous clock that was in almost every photograph of Fleet Street down the years, to replenish the wallet. A bank clerk-like figure would dispense folding money after being shown almost anyone's countersignature on a slip of paper. I christened that corner of the *Telegraph* operation 'the money tree', a description that caught on very quickly.

I mentioned Ken Fleet's delight at tweaking the tail of some financial or industrial bigwig. He did not write all the pieces in his City Editor's column. I sometimes contributed. Fleet was a Liverpudlian. He still had traces of a Scouse accent. Another great Merseysider was the comedian Ken Dodd, with his catchphrase: 'How tickled I am!' The office underlings bet me that I could not get that phrase into Fleet's column. Eventually, commenting on some financial imbroglio, I managed to mould a sentence beginning: 'How tickled I was to see ...' Bet won. Another time, I wrote a piece under Ken Fleet's name making critical comments about doubtful manoeuvres during a takeover battle. There was a Press conference that morning given by the object of my attack. After I had taken my seat, the chairman concerned said he had an important announcement to make. The *Daily Telegraph* City Editor's column had libelled his company, and legal proceedings would be instituted.

Some journalists are eager to be sued, to fight like lions in the courts for truth and suchlike. I have never felt like that, always being sure that if sued, I would be in the wrong, and my mistake would cost my employers dear. Naturally, I always assumed I would be fired. Threats had come on the *Surrey Mirror*, and on the *Standard*, though all had been settled amicably. This latest challenge to my story in the *Telegraph* sounded a lot more serious.

Only a few minutes after the chairman's grim revelation, as I sat and wondered how I would pay the mortgage when no paper would employ me, a chum from the *Financial Times* asked me a most surprising question. Would I like to join the *FT*? Instead of going on the dole, would I be heading for Britain's most respected financial paper? It seemed at that moment most unlikely. In the event, no writ for libel was issued. Soon afterwards I walked the few yards from the back of the *Financial Times* building to an office on the first floor at the front. I was to meet another Fleet Street legend, another one who made me quail.

TEN

Sir Gordon Newton was the man credited with taking the *Financial Times* from a City tip sheet – founded in the late 19th century by that epic swindler, Horatio Bottomley, of all people – to the highly-respected paper it had become by the early 1970s. Newton, a tall, humourless man, was bent over some papers on his desk and barely looked up as I walked in to see him, extremely nervous. Very little was said. He glanced over his half moon glasses. 'Ah, Mr Owen. When can you start?' A flabbergasting way not only to begin a job interview, but more or less end it too. 'Um . . . don't you want to know about me?' I replied.

'No, no,' he flapped a hand. 'I know all about you. Sandy McLachlan has told me all about you. When can you *start?*' He sounded irritated. I babbled about a possible date. 'Any questions?' he snapped. 'Well . . . yes . . . can I ask about . . . you know . . . pay . . .'

'Oh, the managing editor deals with all that. Go and see him. Thank you.' So I joined the staff of the *FT*, on the basis of encouragement from Sandy McLachlan, the pal who had whispered the suggestion at that nerve-wracking Press conference. Nowadays, almost anyone who wants to be taken on by any sort of established employer will almost certainly be put through numerous hoops and probably psychiatric tests. Fleet Street then operated on what I have always thought a sound basis: recommendation.

Here's the oddest thing. Poor old Robin Purdue had taken me on at the *Standard*, but I only served him for a week before his suicide. Gordon Newton had actually retired in the short time between our brief conversation and my starting work at the *FT*. I always took some pleasure from the thought that there was no-one around at either the *Standard* or the *Financial Times* who knew exactly why I had been hired.

It was a thrilling time to be a financial reporter. There was so much going on. A year after I joined, after the Arab-Israeli War of 1973, oil prices shot up, never really to go down much again. Arabs, worsted by the Israelis on the battlefields, had the oil weapon, and used it. Britain lurched from economic crisis to crisis. Company takeovers still made a lot of news. Many famous firms went down. The *FT* newsroom was a frantically busy place, quite unlike the gentlemanly ways of the *Telegraph*. The news editor in charge of the reporters in my early days was the pipe-smoking, no-nonsense Doug Yorke. He looked like Clement Attlee, and used about as many words as the one-time Labour prime minister who had been famous for his brevity. Once Yorke trusted you, there was no end of stories to do. One super day, I got my by-line on the front page of the *Financial Times* on three different pieces. I like to think it is a record that still stands.

A few steps away from Bracken House was the office of Slater Walker, where a financier called Jim Slater did brilliant deals that investors were always clamouring to find out about. Recessions come and recessions go. We chatted once in the midst of a savage downturn set off by the oil crisis. 'In a bust,' Slater said to me, 'no-one can imagine a boom. And in a boom, no-one can imagine a bust.' A line that always comes to mind when the economic cycle has been at one of its extremes.

One of the many byzantine tales I had to cover was the near-demise of one of the country's High Street banks. The drama was to be repeated, only in a much more dangerous way, in the great financial cataclysm of 2008 and 2009. The difference was the extreme caution exercised more than 30 years ago when it came to publishing details of the dodgy state of large banking groups. The one I am thinking of was, actually, bust. Huge efforts were going on behind the scenes to prop it up. Learning what was afoot, I rang the chief executive – managing director tended to be the term then – late one evening. Roused by his wife from his bed, he was extremely grumpy, and refused any comment.

I went to the Editor's office. Newton's successor was a Berlin-born Jew, Fredy Fisher, who had fled the Nazis in the 1930s and served with distinction in the British army before joining the *FT*. I told him of my conversation with the bank boss and what the newsroom had discovered. Fisher sucked on a cigar, bounced his right foot up and down as he so often did – and decided we would refrain from printing anything. All was eventually sorted out discreetly by the Bank of England, a City crisis was averted, and the bank at the centre of all the fuss recovered. Not until 2008 and 2009 would such panics arise again. One difference is that journalists and their editors rush now to reveal news of financial institutions in dire trouble. I am very much in favour of disclosure. I am less sure that it is always such a great idea when important businesses are teetering on the brink of disaster.

The *Financial Times* was a gruelling, marvellously stimulating place to work. Being an *FT* reporter gave you an entree into the most influential City circuits. You met some flamboyant characters, and some downright crooked ones. Firmly in the second category was Robert Maxwell, the Czech-born publisher and sometime Labour MP who ran his dubious empire through a mixture of bluster and creative accounting. No-one apart from the most diligent of financial historians will be interested today in the ins and outs of those old corporate battles. What remains in my memory is dealing with Maxwell himself.

He would go on after my *FT* time to buy the *Daily Mirror* and come to the end of his life in an unexplained drowning off his yacht. He left behind many people whose financial expectations were ruined by his shenanigans, particularly Mirror Group pensioners. I had many encounters with him, when he would bark out his ambitions, make wild forecasts of future profits, and run down anyone opposed to him. After one meeting, when I had tried fruitlessly to get a straight answer out of him on some point at issue during a takeover battle, I returned to the *FT*, to be summoned into the Editor's office. 'I've had Maxwell on the phone,' Fisher said. 'He's furious with you, and demanding we don't print anything about your meeting with him today.' I began to explain the frustrations of dealing with the man. Like so many bullies in the business world, he was fond of threatening legal action. A cool Editor was a great blessing. Fisher waved the usual cigar in my direction. 'Don't worry at all,' he said. 'Carry on and do your story.' It went in the paper just as I wrote it. Not a peep came from Maxwell. No doubt he was arguing with another editor by the time the next issue of the *FT* came out.

Maxwell had always yearned to be a Press baron. Years later, when I had moved into television reporting for Channel Four News and Maxwell had taken control of Mirror Newspapers, he agreed to let me and a camera crew film a morning editorial meeting. He was as bumptious as ever. It was sad to see some of Fleet Street's best editors summoned in, to have their ideas derided by the biggest scoundrel since Horatio Bottomley.

If the *Telegraph* of the 1970s had been reluctant to publish things unkind to the Conservatives, the *Financial Times* had a reputation for timidity in digging out new stories. Journalists should relish being able to reveal what is really going on. The *FT* was not on the whole very brave. It could be sometimes. I was set the difficult task of trying to unravel how a Far East shipping tycoon called Ravi Tikkoo managed to find the money to buy and sail a fleet of oil tankers which were the biggest on the planet. There was no suggestion, I should add, that anything illegal was involved. I paid for a lunch in a gloomy City restaurant and pumped a merchant banking contact for information on how it was all possible. It had much to do with 'tax shelters' – less politely, how to exploit loopholes in tax regimes in one country or another.

Tikkoo himself was expansive and terribly friendly when I went to talk to him. Friendly and unforthcoming. Finally I put together a feature which tried to chart the clever ways the shipping magnate employed to run his ships. Almost inevitably, Tikkoo was furious, and his lawyers were quickly in touch, talking of frightful inaccuracies and warning of libel writs. A lengthy apology had to be printed. That should have been mortifying for an *FT* person, considering the paper's reputation for accurate reporting of reams of facts, unadventurous as most of the stuff filling its pink columns tended to be. It is another tribute to Fredy Fisher's faith in his staff that it was never suggested I should be hauled in to be reprimanded.

There were other occasions when the *FT* did break news. As the first oil price shock hit the UK, and Britain's underlying economic weakness was cruelly exposed, Ted Heath's Tory government was forced to order a three-day working week to conserve energy supplies. As the economy stalled, some businesses began to fall apart. There was a big commercial property company called Lyon, based in south London, which struggled for weeks to get its creditors to allow it time to get its finances in order as the property market dived. Day after day, a key figure within the company decided to keep me informed of the twists and turns as his fellow executives sweated to stay afloat. Very satisfying for me. Less so for the company's boss, Ronnie Lyon, a property developer renowned for his love of flashy yachts and expensive cars.

Another extraordinary character, though not an outrightly criminal one like Robert Maxwell, was 'Tiny' Rowland, who ran a rambling outfit called Lonrho. It was based largely on mining interests in Africa, and a lot of its business dealings did not bear overmuch scrutiny. Rowland was a large, fleshy man who intimidated his boardroom rivals with the same sort of bullying that Maxwell employed. One of his non-executive directors, an old retired senior Army officer who clearly took a dim view of this Rowland chap, decided to whisper down the phone to me many of the secrets that passed across the boardroom table. They produced more of the front page stories that reporters crave: exclusives that have other papers scrambling to catch up.

Ted Heath, the Prime Minister, became so exasperated with Lonrho's activities that he uttered the memorable phrase in the House of Commons that the company and 'Tiny' Rowland represented the 'unacceptable face of capitalism'. I wrote the story which led the next morning's *FT*.

The world of finance and business usually preoccupied us. Sometimes, though, we got caught up in wider and often violent events. An early afternoon's work in 1973 was interrupted by another loud thump – after Northern Ireland I could recognise a bomb blast – and the tall windows beside my desk vibrated violently. The IRA had planted a car bomb a few hundred yards away, close to the Old Bailey. If there was any warning, it was useless. It was a crowded spot, and nearly two hundred people were injured. One man died.

For most of my working life I have lived in east Surrey. A few miles away is Caterham, which used to be home to the headquarters of the Grenadier Guards. In the summer of 1975 yet another IRA bomb blew up the Caterham Arms pub just across the road from the Guards' barracks. The *FT* rang to send me off to find out what had happened. There had been no warning. This time I stood in a familiar street on the UK mainland to witness things that seemed completely unreal. More than 30 people were injured, many of them soldiers, and many were very badly hurt. It made a story on the pink front page of the *Financial Times* very different from my usual ones.

After several years of financial reporting, I requested a change, and spent an exhilarating period on the Men and Matters diary column. Newspaper diarists are the gadflies of the trade, able to ask the impertinent and off-beat questions that more serious-minded hacks avoid. On the *FT* that meant digging out the odder tales from the often obscure world of business. And not always business. Occasionally we would lurch into politics, if there seemed an intriguing story line. One evening I was in the lobby of the House of Commons, chatting to some senior Conservatives as they awaited the result of a ballot to decide who would succeed Ted Heath as their leader. When it was announced that Margaret Thatcher had triumphed, it was fascinating to see the pure shock on the faces of those top male Tories. Geoffrey Howe, who would become Thatcher's Chancellor before finally breaking very publicly with her, gazed down at his shoes. Ahead for him, Thatcher, and the rest of the party was an election victory in 1979 that would keep them in power for almost two decades.

On the Men and Matters column I was immensely lucky to work at first with a classic diary writer, Quentin Guirdham. With spectacles perched on the end of his nose, he had a certain otherworldliness that belied a keen intelligence. He regarded deadlines as things that could be treated with a certain insouciance. That tended to annoy everyone from the Editor to the printers. Guirdham was forgiven, because his pen was sharp, his journalism often golden.

There was another catch to working with him. He had promised a publisher or two to produce a book. In fact, I think advances had been paid. He had already co-edited *The London Spy: A Discreet Guide to the City's Pleasures*, published in 1971. The trouble was dear Guirdham never quite had the time to compile another book. Very often I would be in our small office on the north west corner of Bracken House – with a commanding and often distracting view of London's greatest glory, St Paul's Cathedral – when a querulous publisher would come on the phone, demanding to speak to his author. I would mutter about an urgent appointment which had called Mr Guirdham away, making empty promises that the call would be returned.

Putting the diary together included the task of going down to the 'stone'. In the hot, noisy *FT* composing room were the large tables where the metal type was laid into page-sized frames. The effect was to produce metallic mirror images of the pages to be printed. You had to get used to reading the type backwards, being prepared to write some extra lines if copy fell short, or to have some snappy ideas about what to cut if you had written too much. My time on the stone at the local paper was good experience. It had taught the importance of calculating accurately the amount of words needed so that the whole printing process was not held up. The one danger was actually going anywhere close to touching the metal. That was a print worker's job, and in those old, unreconstructed Fleet Street days, it would be 'everybody out' and the tight print schedule would be wrecked.

It was to be a few more years before Rupert Murdoch took on the print unions as new technology helped him sweep away their dictatorships over the production of national newspapers.

Another hazard of the diary column was to deal with the day's cartoon. We used the talented Ken Mahood, a gentle Northern Irishman who would go on to a distinguished career drawing for the *Daily Mail* until his retirement at the end of 2009. The routine was that Ken would do rough outlines of three or four cartoons with their captions. The difficulty was that the choice of the one to be printed was supposed to fall to the Editor, Fredy Fisher. His Teutonic roots did not give him much appreciation of British humour. I would take Mahood's offerings into the Editor's sanctum. Our German-born boss would hum, haw, thump his leg up and down, drop ash from his eternal cigar, and usually ask: 'What is funny about this one? Or that one?' And so on. Nothing drains humour out of a cartoon faster than having to explain it. Often, Fisher would wave Ken Mahood's efforts away, leaving the choice to me.

Quentin Guirdham died unexpectedly, not many years later. As his friends, family and old colleagues like me went into his memorial service in St Bride's just off Fleet Street – the 'journalists' church' – there was a large photograph of one of the best writers among so many classy ones I have known. There was the mischievous grin. And there were the specs, hovering as always right on the end of his nose. The publisher never did get his book.

Quentin Guirdham's departure from Men and Matters opened the door for another colleague. A highly-respected one in his best days, he had fallen foul of the drink. Sandy McLachlan had been the *FT* man who had whispered to me that there was a job on his paper if I wanted it. When the Editor told me McLachlan would be replacing Guirdham, I was alarmed. Diary work is fun. It is also unforgivingly relentless. A workmate too fond of booze would be a nightmare. Fredy Fisher didn't disagree. He thought the discipline of a daily column would, literally, sober Sandy up. A generous if vain hope. McLachlan would always start the morning brimming with ideas. Once a long lunch had been taken, most of the brilliant thoughts had slithered away.

It was time for another change. I went to the news desk, to the central newsgathering unit. I cannot say it was the most enjoyable job. It was, however, where I experienced the sort of kindness that the usually rough world of national newspapers could occasionally show. A case in point was Sandy McLachlan, my last Men and Matters colleague, being offered the chance of a job it was hoped would save him. As it happened, it did not, and he died soon afterwards.

ELEVEN

From a television presenter's chair in my sixties I look back with admiration at the journalist I used to be. To deal day after day with the most complex issues under intense deadline pressures for the most exacting of newspapers is not something I could manage now. There was a personal price to pay.

After ten years, my marriage to Philippa unravelled. The demands of work had not helped. Divorce is almost always an agonising experience, made worse if there are children. We had two. Rebecca had been born in 1969, Anthony was adopted in 1976. Philippa went off to live with, and soon marry, another guy. I was utterly determined not to lose touch with my children. Good friends rescued me from the worst miseries and often provided somewhere I could take Rebecca and her little brother. Richard and Cynthia Feast I have known since we were all still in our late teens. Valerie Golden was another to whom I owe so much. Her own much worse agony would come some years later with the suicide of her young son Dominic.

Chums at the *Financial Times* were endlessly sympathetic too. Having learned that Philippa wanted our marriage ended, I took a couple of days off before returning to the news desk. The man in charge, David Walker, took me in hand. There was to be no work done by me. I was marched to the pub, filled with drink until I could barely stand, and sent home. The perfect way to deal with the crisis.

A great opportunity came my way a few months later. After five years at the *FT* you could take a sabbatical. The idea was to go away for a month and soak yourself in some subject, or place, to broaden the journalistic mind. Through a girl friend's contacts I could stay for a while in South Africa. As my plane lifted off from Heathrow, I looked down as the clouds gradually blotted out the familiar British landscape. It was clear that it was a time for a new life.

Certainly visiting South Africa in the late 1970s was an extraordinary way to begin. Apartheid ruled. Most of the rest of the world professed to disapprove, and sometimes in that amazing month, the country did its best to convince me that the unflattering image was well deserved. There was the PR man who took me to lunch in a smart club in Johannesburg – white diners waited on by black staff, naturally – who talked about the controversies being stirred up by a newspaper which was liberal by the South African standards of the day. 'Mr Owen,' my host drawled in the scratchy, guttural accent of those parts, 'do you know what is wrong with the *Rand Daily Mail*?' No, I did not. 'Mr Owen . . . the black man reads the *Rand Daily Mail*!'

The separation of the races ordained by the Apartheid rules could be brutal. They could also be farcical. I became a victim. One bright morning, I waited at a stop to get on a Johannesburg trolleybus. It was probably one that had started out as a London trolley before being exported second hand. Once inside, I could have been on a journey back home. Except as I looked round, I realised every passenger was black. A large black bus inspector bore down on me. Outraged, he told me because I was white I was not allowed on board. The trolleybus made an emergency stop, and I was turfed off.

The shanty towns around Johannesburg and Cape Town told their own clear stories of how so many of South Africa's people had to live. Even more difficult were the conditions for those employed in the gold mines, the country's main source of wealth. Thanks to coming from the *Financial Times*, there was an invitation to have a look inside one. Plummeting to one of the deepest in the world was an incredible experience. And almost a fatal one for me. I was taken about ten thousand feet below ground at the Western Deep mine. Once the cage had reached the bottom, I started walking, then had to crawl for several hundred yards over broken rock through a tunnel only slightly taller and wider than my own scrabbling body. At the end, a black miner was on all fours, carefully fixing explosive to blast away the next few yards of solid rock to get at the tiny slivers of gold. It was unbearably hot.

Having seen the man at work with his dynamite, I and the mining official escorting me crawled back towards the bottom of the shaft. When I got there, I felt dreadful. I was more dizzy and nauseous than I had ever known. I was shaking, and almost oblivious to my surroundings. I could not quite work out whether I was very hot or freezing cold. My escort took off his white safety hat, using it to scoop up water cascading down the walls of the shaft. He poured hatful after hatful over me. As I revived slowly, he told me cheerfully I had most of the symptoms of heat exhaustion. I had been close to collapse.

After we reached the surface, and walked out in the sunshine, I felt better. Good enough to enjoy a fine lunch in the directors' dining room, where the economics of the gold business were explained. They depended to a great extent on the migrant labourers who came from other parts of Africa, leaving behind their families to stay in huge and unlovely hostels. And be paid pretty poorly to do the hideously dirty and dangerous work far underground. Well away from the directors' groaning lunch table. I mused on what I had seen and heard as I drove back to Johannesburg. I did not have much opportunity to enjoy the gorgeous mountain scenery en route. Rich food on top of heat exhaustion was not an ideal combination. I had to pull over a couple of times, hang out of the car – and be violently sick.

The scariest experience of the month-long visit actually came somewhere other than South Africa. It happened in the so-called homeland of Swaziland, a poor patch of countryside surrounded by the dominant Republic of South Africa, which allowed the little kingdom to run most of its own affairs. I was driving along one of its severely potholed roads when I was stopped by a bunch of Swazi soldiers. They pointed guns and shouted at me. They were quite obviously drunk. There was a young officer a few steps away, and I asked as firmly as I could for him to come forward. The tension rose. I reached very, very slowly into an inside pocket. It was the old cinematic cliché. Was he going for a gun? No, I was going for my British passport. I flourished it in their faces, spoke sternly, and repeated a word that has saved many a journalist's bacon across the globe. 'BBC! BBC!' Even later on, when I worked for the BBC's greatest commercial television rival, that was a standby at times of peril. Having survived my encounter, I discovered later that some South African tourists had been shot and wounded on the same stretch of road.

It was not the end of all the hazards of Swaziland. As I drove along another dirt track that passed for a major road out of the fly-blown capital of Mbabane towards the nearest border with South Africa proper, a large policeman flagged me down. 'Speeding,' he mumbled, fingering a large pistol. I understood at once. A wad of South African rand notes was peeled off, handed over, and I was waved on.

There were other vivid moments. Marvelling at the world's biggest diamond mine, in Kimberley. Seeing Table Mountain and Cape Town for the first time, sweeping in on the plane from Johannesburg. Motoring across the Karoo, the beautiful empty middle of South Africa under the biggest sky imaginable. And taking my hire car many miles down a dirt road to Cape Agulhas, the southernmost tip of Africa, where shipwrecked hulks rear up as you near the coast, and where I walked out of a dingy and unpleasant hotel having tried and failed to eat some appallingly nasty locally-caught fish.

Politics and the impact of Apartheid were never far away. Over an evening meal with journalist friends I listened as a mixed race writer discussed what was so wrong about the government and what it did to its black people. As the conversation ended, my host reminded me that our dinner companion could be locked up for expressing such views in public. Small revenges can be very satisfying. I flew home on a South African Airways plane. The service aboard was correct though not very friendly. The aircraft taxied to a stop some way from the terminals at Heathrow. SAA planes were thought of as potential targets then. At the bottom of the gangway, two buses waited to get us to the airport buildings. One was already full and standing. I made for the other, empty one. 'You must board the first bus,' snapped a stewardess in that South African twang. I smiled: 'I'm not in *your* country now. I'll take the second bus, thank you.'

Once back at the *Financial Times* I was restless. One quiet afternoon, the phone rang on the news desk. It was a man called Patrick Hutber, little remembered now but a towering journalistic figure in his day. He had been City Editor of the *Sunday Telegraph*, and wielded considerable influence over those who followed his wisdom on the doings of the financial markets. He coined a great phrase: 'Improvement means deterioration'. If you think something is being re-designed to make it better . . . chances are, you are wrong. The words are often quoted. Few today would know who originated them.

Hutber had left the *Telegraph* having been recruited by Sir James Goldsmith, a swashbuckling business tycoon almost as famous for his colourful personal life as his financial achievements. He had also coined a phrase on a subject in which he could claim expertise: 'When a man marries his mistress he creates a vacancy.' His daughter Jemima would eventually marry, and then divorce, the Pakistani cricketer and sometime politician Imran Khan.

Goldsmith had decided to start a news magazine along the lines of the American *Time* and *Newsweek* titles. Such ventures had never flourished in Britain, so well served by national newspapers. Goldsmith was

73

determined to have a go. He was motivated not only by what he saw as a business possibility but also by determination to have a loud voice in public affairs. It got him into head-on conflict with the likes of *Private Eye*, whose writers ridiculed him and anyone who wanted to work for him. The magazine was to be called *Now!* – not to be confused at all with a much later gossipy title of the same name – and be published weekly. It would use the latest technology and run lots of colour pictures. Old-fashioned printing processes, and old-fashioned printers, would not be needed. All very revolutionary for the late 1970s.

Private Eye dubbed the magazine 'Talbot', after a British-made car notorious for its poor performance. Anyone accepting a job at *Now!* was scorned and said to be taking the 'Marmite shilling,' a slighting reference to one of Goldsmith's food companies. Goldsmith wanted the best journalists, people who would be willing to brave the widespread hostility to him and his plans. They would be well rewarded.

Patrick Hutber was not a man to be put off by the pinpricks of criticism. As Business Editor he and *Now!*'s chosen Editor, Tony Shrimsley, were Goldsmith's principal lieutenants and recruiting sergeants, offering those Marmite shillings. The phone call to me began with Hutber saying: 'I want you to be my deputy.' I was not at all sure, well aware of the sniping at Goldsmith and his pugnacious attitudes. 'I'll double your salary,' Hutber went on. 'You don't know,' I replied, 'what my salary is!'

'Doesn't matter. Whatever it is, I'll double it.'

After seven years on the *FT* I accepted on the spot. A safe billet swapped for an uncertain one, even if it came with a comfortable price tag. This was certain to be an adventure. The next couple of years were a whirl of new personal and professional experiences. Patrick Hutber was like no-one else I had ever worked for. I discovered quickly that accuracy with numbers was not his major forte. Surprising perhaps in a man who had such a high reputation as a City writer. Millions and billions could easily get confused. One of my prime responsibilities was to spot any numerate infelicities in his otherwise sparkling copy.

James Goldsmith was the flamboyant type, and Hutber could be as well. He had two cars, a Bentley and a sports job. His idea of lunch was to set off in the Bentley for his club, leaving the swanky motor on a yellow line outside the front door of the Garrick. I learned that it was pointless suggesting he might get a parking ticket. He never seemed to.

Tony Shrimsley was a very tough Editor, having come from similar roles in Fleet Street. He succeeded in gathering around him some big stars of the trade, attracted – like me – by the money on offer. Not only that, we were guaranteed a year's salary if *Now!* went down. Geoffrey Howe, the politician who had studied his shoes closely that night in the Commons when Mrs Thatcher had become Tory leader, was a reform-minded Chancellor of the Exchequer. One of his popular measures among the better-off was to lift the tax-exempt limit on redundancy payouts to £30,000. At our generous salary levels, that made *Now!* personnel relaxed about any closure.

Before issue number one, Goldsmith invited us to his palatial home at Ham in south west London. It might have been billed as a dinner. It was more like a banquet. The tables were very long, the room cavernous. The lighting was subdued and flickery, adding to the dramatic atmosphere. Amid the excited chatter, our ebullient tycoon got to his feet to tell us how wonderful this new publication was going to be. He had great charm, and he could inspire. It felt like we were being led into a medieval battle, with food and wine galore and loud acclamation for every confident forecast from our great leader.

I never had any time for Robert Maxwell, and was always very glad I never worked for him or other turbo-charged billionaires like Tiny Rowland. But I admit that Goldsmith beguiled me. He was no crook, though I am sure he sailed as close to stormy winds as he could. What he could also do was sweep you along with his unstoppable enthusiasm. All very different from the measured, careful world of the *Financial Times*. *Now!*'s office was just north of the scruffy Old Street roundabout between the City of London and Islington. The magazine looked good, with colour splashed through it – unusual for those days, remember – punctuating journalism of high quality.

Hutber was a joy to be with, if very unpredictable. For the business news, we got together a small but impressive team. Bill Kay, a highly reliable producer of stories, joined from the *Evening News*. Eamonn Fingleton was a sometimes brooding but always highly intelligent writer. Colleen Toomey was another recruit from the *FT*, full of fun and hard-working. Hutber's wayward habits with figures persuaded him and me that we needed a 'number cruncher'. A young David Smith, later to become the *Sunday Times*'s highly-regarded Economics Editor, came along. Lots of us smoked in the office. David chose a pipe. As he says in middle age, his hope had been to make himself look older and wiser.

Outside our little empire, the *Now!* newsroom throbbed with highly-strung and often frightening personalities. The news editor under Shrimsley was Brian Hitchen, a rough and tumble operator of the old Fleet Street school, who scared the hell out of most of his staff. Because we were published near the end of the week, the production cycle meant we had a big editorial conference every Sunday morning. The lynx-eyed, short-tempered editor Tony Shrimsley would grill department heads, demanding to know why we were not ahead on this story or that. Hitchen would smile broadly, promising great things, and preparing to fire rockets at those who were not performing to order. Woe betide you if your menu of pieces did not sound spicy enough. Hitchen had a much calmer, almost sleepy sidekick, who week after week would suggest we ought to be investigating a threat of invasion by 'killer bees'. I don't think the story ever ran, or the bees ever flew in.

Later on, I would tumble into the different environment of television news. Very competitive? Yes, of course. Yet not nearly so demanding or uncomfortably nasty as most national newspapers, or outfits like *Now!*. TV people are on the whole very nice. Not a word that would sum up Fleet Street and its occupants. The crash and bang of colliding egos was only one of my difficulties at the magazine. The other was having two small children to look after at weekends, the story of divorced fathers everywhere. There was no choice but to take them to the Old Street office, plonk them down with lots of paper, pens and crayons, and occasionally get them something to eat or drink. Hard on the nerves, for me and for Rebecca and Anthony.

For the first few months, Goldsmith's influence was imperceptible. His many enemies had assumed he would use *Now!* to push his right-wing views. For a long time, he left the journalism to the journalists. I had one curious conversation with him. *Now!*'s owner and that other business beast Tiny Rowland of Lonrho hated one another. Some ancient financial feud no doubt accounted for it. One Sunday, Goldsmith rang and told me a long tale of some mischief that he claimed Rowland was mixed up in. At the end of the conversation, I pointed out to my employer that what he had said was potentially highly libellous. His account could not simply go in the magazine without our lawyers going through it. And binning it, I was sure. On the other hand, Goldsmith was in charge. He could in theory do what he liked. Goldsmith said, not very helpfully, that it was up to me to decide. Hutber was not around. He tended to leave the inconvenient Sundays to me. So I alerted Editor Shrimsley. He waved me away. The dirt on Rowland was never dished, and I never heard another word about it.

Goldsmith's foes were unrelenting in their sneery criticisms. *Private Eye* delighted in reporting how poorly sales were doing. As the circulation drifted downwards, Goldsmith began commissioning articles more to his quite extreme political tastes. The bile from the *Eye* and others grew accordingly. All was not helped by an economy struggling out of the doldrums of the 1970s. We were always woefully short of advertising. The magazine's gloss, and the writing of the likes of Frank Johnson, a genius of a political satirist, could not hide the truth that we were doomed.

A dreadful tragedy would come before the inevitable collapse. The Christmas period of 1980 was chilly, and many roads were treacherous. Hutber set off to spend the seasonal break at his large house a good way from London in rural Buckinghamshire. He was in his sports car rather than the Bentley. Not far from home he lost control and crashed. Horribly injured, he was brought back to Bart's Hospital in London, where I would go to see him, deeply unconscious and draped in tubes.

He never woke, and his death was a terrible blow for those he had persuaded to join him for the *Now!* adventure. My colleagues in the business department were appalled. Their sadness was mixed with despair for a future without Hutber. We had all felt privileged to work for him. We all knew he had been our protection from some of the wilder spirits at Old Street. My admiration for those colleagues knew no bounds when they all agreed to stay on.

Patrick Hutber was irreplaceable in the sense of anyone of his stature, or anywhere near it, being willing to take their chances with the floundering *Now!* magazine. Tony Shrimsley summoned me to say I was to be the new Business Editor. As so often with my editors, a curious exchange followed. He explained that a car came with the title. Thank you, I said. Er . . . what sort of car? A Ford Granada. More thanks as I left his office, wondering what a Ford Granada was like. I wandered round some car parks until I saw one. They were big machines. Very ritzy compared to the sort of jalopies I was used to. Suddenly, I would be driving an upmarket, claret-coloured luxury motor. And all maintenance and repairs would be someone else's responsibility.

I only had a few months to enjoy running the car and my office – never again would I have my own desk, deep carpets, use of my own fridge, plus attentive secretary – before *Now!*'s inevitable closure. The end had its comic touches. At the usual Sunday conference, the one that would turn out to be the last, Tony Shrimsley was uncharacteristically relaxed, offering no criticisms at all as stories significant and trivial were discussed. The next day, his lack of rigour was explained. Mid-morning, he stood on a chair in the newsroom and announced we could not go on. I knew what I had to do. I made straight for the lift, went into the office car park, and whisked the claret Granada away. I knew security would be quick to lock the staff car park. I spent a week or so cruising around, visiting friends, and filling up my gas guzzler using a *Now!* credit card.

I watched as the by-lines of *Now!* writers began turning up in other places. I was in no hurry to be employed again. In the summer of 1981, I did some freelance sub-editing for my old paper, the *Financial Times*, enjoying the much easier time that you could have away from the high pressures of reporting. One evening, with some *FT* colleagues, I went for a stroll past St Paul's Cathedral, stepping round the crowds gathered along the pavements for a big event the following day: the wedding of the Prince of Wales and Diana Spencer. One day, they would play an enormous part in my working life. All I knew that year was that I wanted a big change.

Apart from *Now!*'s turbulent days and demise, my father had died, and divorce still hurt like mad. Among the *Now!* employees had been a friendly man called Jon Lander. Unlike most of the Old Street crew, he was easy-going, and we talked often about where he had come from. He had been a correspondent for Independent Television News. I began to plot a change of direction.

There was one postscript to the 19 months at *Now!*. A few days after the closure, the staff had queued up to get their fat redundancy cheques. Weeks later a letter arrived from the liquidators of the communication company within the Goldsmith empire that had formally controlled the magazine. It informed me that owing to a clerical error I had been overpaid by a few pounds and pence. Would I please send a cheque to return the money? It was one of the few occasions when I could sit down and with good cheer write a note with a short yet clear message. 'Dear Sir. Thank you for your letter of . . . Fuck Off. Yours sincerely . . .'

TWELVE

Getting up early is something I have always found hard. Strange, therefore, to wonder about being a milkman. I did consider it seriously enough to take an exam at the local dairy. If someone orders three pints of gold top on Monday, two of blue top on Wednesday, and an orange juice being sold at a discount on Friday, what would the bill at the end of the week be? The supervisor told me I had scored the best marks of any applicant he had known. As a change of direction, it would have been a violent swerve. I thought I fancied a job where most of my time would be my own. It was only a fleeting ambition. Just as well. Doorstep milk deliveries have been disappearing fast. The dairy near my home at Reigate in Surrey, where I have lived on or off for nearly half a century, shut not so long after I sat my test there.

Back to television. I had long thought about being a TV reporter. To get on the box was something I wanted more and more. Anyone who appears, in whatever role, is giving a performance. And performing was a great love. There had been lots of amateur acting, squeezed in among the long hours of newspaper and magazine work, to say nothing of pursuing a great interest in railways. Memories of theatrical fun include getting an award as the best amateur actor in south east England in 1977, thanks to a jolly, short play by A.P. Herbert called *Two Gentlemen of Soho*. I was required to die in Shakespearean style, in other words at great and verbose length. My award-winning night started badly. I had decided to wear for the part some two-tone shoes, with substantial heels. They were uncomfortable if fashionably popular in the late 1970s. As makeup was being applied, as my nerves jangled unbearably, I realised I had left the vital footwear at home. It was a 16-mile round trip, done at breakneck speed, to get the two-tones. I went on stage pretty flustered.

For my dying speech, A.P. Herbert had imitated the Bard's way of reeling off names of important allies. He replaced the 'Buckingham, and

Show-off: with the cup for Best Actor, 1977.

fair Suffolk' approach with a string of London station names. With my intimate knowledge of the capital's termini, I could gasp them out in any order, useful for a poor learner of lines. 'Alas, poor Waterloo and Euston . . .' (heavy breathing for a pause) '. . . and dear Blackfriars, Kings Cross and Paddington . . .' It did not matter whether I spoke the playwright's lines exactly, the trick was to maintain the rhythm until the final collapse in death. It may sound corny. It worked so well, I got the cup.

More than 30 years later I became involved with another local drama festival, and with it the chance to meet one of the best screen actors Britain's ever produced. Sir Michael Caine has been the star supporter of the Leatherhead festival. In 2011 he was not available as usual to appear on the stage on the last night to present the prizes and say a few words of congratulation and encouragement. If Caine couldn't be there, would I step in for him? I agreed, if rather daunted. It was also agreed that I would meet him at his Surrey home nearby, to video a quick chat about the festival's importance which could be shown on that last night. We sat together on a bench in his garden, and before the filming began we chatted about our common backgrounds. We both came from families in south London whose menfolk had worked in the old produce

80

Old Londoners: a chat with Sir Michael Caine. (Picture by Andy Newbold Photography)

81

markets. To hear his so-familiar cockney drawl as he remembered *his* grandparents' generation was marvellous.

Back in the 1970s, there were many memorable theatrical moments. There was a round of applause even before I opened my mouth as Humphrey Bogart in Woody Allen's gorgeous *Play It Again, Sam*. The raincoat, tilted hat, and cigarette looked just right. What a treat to growl priceless lines like 'I never met a dame who did not understand a slap in the mouth, or a slug from a 45.' Hardly wonderful for the confidence was one stagehand who whispered in my ear 'I wouldn't go out there for a million quid' just before I went on to open a revue with a stand-up comedy routine. Stage fright was total. The jokes went fine.

'Ah, you are a bit of a thespian,' people often say, as if somehow one should be shy of admitting it. Not at all. Applause is wonderful when it sweeps over you. Laughter is better still. For a 'thesp' I once made a very interesting discovery, though. I played the Gentleman Caller in Tennessee Williams's *The Glass Menagerie*. A dark, difficult play. A few days into the run, my father died in hospital in Brighton after a miserable year or so with pancreatic cancer. I rang the play's producer. I said I would be there for that night's show, although I would probably be below par. I felt I was sleep-walking through the evening, as if in a trance. Lines came almost robotically. Afterwards, I was told it was my best performance. I know it was.

I hope my dear Dad, such an enthusiastic actor himself once, would have understood. After the Navy, he worked for Rothschilds, the City merchant bank, for about 30 years. Towards the end, before he retired – he would only live another year afterwards – he admitted to me he had become disillusioned with his working life. That I have wanted to avoid at all costs. And the acting pushed me to find a way to perform, and be paid for it.

I had a lovely bit of early television experience when I presented a few editions of *What The Papers Say*, Granada TV's long-running series looking at what the Press was up to. The routine was to catch a train to Manchester, clutching a pile of several days' worth of newspapers, having selected cuttings and headlines that had caught the eye.

Once in Granada's studio, the show was recorded 'as live', in other words without stops and starts. The presenter would introduce a cutting and it would be read out by one of a handful of actors sitting round a table. After each cutting, it was back to the presenter for a comment. Being at work with professional performers was a treat. One stumbled a bit over his words. We bashed on, and there was no suggestion of a re-take to correct the slight imperfection. When we listened to the playback, the old actor who had 'tripped' smiled genially at his colleagues: 'We'll call it "drop out", eh?' 'Drop out' is the expression used for a technical hitch on a sound track.

The *What The Papers Say* treat was enormously enhanced because one of the readers was Daphne Oxenford. As a small child I had heard her reading, in her crystal clear voice, stories on the radio programme *Listen With Mother*. A big name in my house, she was. It was disconcerting to go the bar afterwards and hear the legend ask if I would mind buying her a large gin and tonic.

After my first *What the Papers Say* Quentin Guirdham who had been such a superb if rather under-organised fellow writer on the *Financial Times* diary column sent me a letter. He said he was sure that in doing television, I had found the thing I would be really good at. One very pleasing part of it all was that my father saw those early TV moments.

In the middle of 1981 I decided that I would pursue broadcasting properly. I have often told young people desperate to scramble somehow into the overcrowded world of TV and radio that my route could not possibly be copied today. Thirty or so years ago the BBC had an Appointments Department just across the road from Broadcasting House, its headquarters in London's Portland Place. I went in and behind a counter was a pleasant and helpful lady. It was like being in an old-fashioned shop. 'I'd like to work for the BBC,' I told her. She, having no idea who I was, replied: 'Oh. What do you do?' Fortunately I used a key word in reply. 'I'm a journalist.' That set bells ringing and she opened a filing cabinet drawer to pull out some papers. 'There's a vacancy for a Regional Journalist at the newsroom in Newcastle Upon Tyne. Would you be interested?'

Why not? I was out of work. I had the *Now!* redundancy money keeping me afloat. Personal life may have been in tatters but it did mean there was freedom to chase any fancied rainbow. Always, I tell aspiring young broadcasters and anyone else who cares to listen, if a door is a quarter open, always go through it. Opportunities untried can only bring regrets.

I drove the 250 miles or so to the North East, an area I hardly knew. The bosses of BBC regional news on Tyneside did not know quite what to make of me. They asked a couple of important questions. What was the political make-up of their area? Quite easy: Labour almost had a stranglehold. What were the leading football teams? I had no real idea.

They were good enough to accept I would probably not cover much sport. It was pointed out that the reality of working as a Regional Journalist behind the scenes might not appeal. I might not be any good. A six-month contract, without pension rights, was agreed. At a salary that was about a quarter of what James Goldsmith had paid me.

My new boss was John Bird, a Cumbrian-born news man devoted to his station. His deputy, who handed out the tasks in the newsroom, was a Scotsman called Ronnie Burns. His journalistic background included that brutal old school, the *Scottish Daily Express*. He could be a gruff, even frightening figure. His heart was really made of gold, once you got to know him. It was sad to see his health collapse years later, and to visit him in an overcrowded hospital in south London, where he died.

A couple of days after I started, I went out with one of the reporters on a story. Tony Baker is one of those experts who makes the business look deceptively easy. A regional TV reporter always had his or her hands full. They had to deal with the cameraman and soundman, think of sensible questions to ask interviewees, write the commentary, often record it in the back of a car or in a street, finally send back to the studio pictures and words that would be stitched together for transmission. I knew straight away that was what I wanted to do.

The BBC in the North East was still using film. One magazine would last about nine minutes before it needed changing. You had to avoid shooting too much. And you had to remember that it took three-quarters of an hour to get the film through the 'bath', as the developing process was called. It could be speeded up and ready in half an hour, except the pictures would come out rather yellow. Learning the technicalities was arduous. Out 'on the road' you had to foresee clearly how the eventual piece would appear on air. Tony Baker and the other North East reporters made it look easy.

On an early outing, I despatched film and commentary back to Newcastle, arriving at the studio after the regional evening news programme, *Look North*, had gone out. The film editor who had received my roadside offerings hailed me as I walked past his cubbyhole. He spun through the several minutes of film. Then he played my sound track. They hardly related to each other at all. His job had been made impossible. A big lesson learned.

The editor was Howard Perks, who settled in the West Country to be an independent film maker. Years later we would go together one winter to a stone cold Sarajevo, to make a programme about the former Liberal leader Paddy Ashdown who was then in charge of Bosnia. Howard is a gifted film maker. Some of my clearest and most haunting Sarajevo memories, however, came from walking alone around that sad but thrilling city. I tracked my way to the bridge where the shots were fired that sparked World War One, then up to the heights where the Serb forces rained down murderous fire on civilians during Bosnia's civil war. Another walk out of the city took me to a depot – even in Sarajevo a transport enthusiast could find something fascinating – where tramcars damaged by sniping and shell and mortar fire were lined up, a dismal parade of battered survivors.

In Newcastle, because of my financial background, I was often on the big industrial stories of the day. It was a hugely significant time for what has always been an employment blackspot. The once mighty shipyards along the Tyne and the Wear were in decline. It was strange for a soft Southerner to film hordes of men leaving the Swan Hunter yard at the end of a shift, to see them scuttling up the hill that led away from their workplace. It was a ritual that could have been witnessed any time in the previous hundred years. It could not last. Foreign competition would soon kill the old shipyards.

Terminal decline loomed too for the other staple industry of the North East: the coal mines. Many of them stretched out under the North Sea. So many men would have to look for other jobs. Many would never find any. And it was not just shipbuilding and mining that were contracting fast. Manufacturers large and small were being squeezed out. I arrived at one small factory with my camera crew to interview the boss. As I walked up the path to the entrance, an employee came past, and muttered in the Geordie accent I had such difficulty understanding in my early North East days: 'Ah . . . if you're here, then we must be doomed.' It was hard sometimes to reconcile my knowledge of the harsh realities of market places and economics with the difficulties that were thrust upon men and families who had always accepted that hard graft was their lot. And who were then devastated to be told there was no future for what they did.

The big stories, and the hardest moments for local reporters, came with the miners' strike which broke out in early 1984. Foggy, freezing early mornings on picket lines outside collieries could be very uncomfortable assignments. Quietly-spoken threats to journalists were common. One large, glowering pitman whispered in my ear that if the camera was turned on, I would find myself tipped over the nearest wall. I went and complained to an equally large police sergeant. He turned away. He

85

was a local man. He probably lived in the next street to the miner who would gladly have flattened me.

Another time, I found myself in the middle of a group of young mineworkers, my age and under. They were grousing about the way the media was portraying them. They wanted to be back at work, and they also wanted promises that the Government would not press ahead with mass pit closures. Which is what their union leaders, especially the fiery Arthur Scargill, had told them. As we talked, I asked if they really wanted their sons to go down the pit one day, to labour away in the dark and dirt for their whole lives. The reluctant answer was No. What else would those sons do, though?

Scargill was dead right about the Government's intentions. He was also a horror to deal with. At an evening rally in Durham, the heart of the North East mining community, he addressed a crowd of strikers. The BBC were there. He turned at one point, and waved his finger towards me and my camera crew. 'There's your enemy!' he bellowed. It was only the great good sense and courtesy of those angry Durham men that saved us from a punch-up.

The police sergeant who had ignored my complaining made a deep impression. I became increasingly uncomfortable with the way Margaret Thatcher's government – who would amply fulfil Scargill's prophecy of the near death of British coal mining – deployed police from all Britain to confront the strikers. The sights of coppers massed beside motorways to turn back flying pickets were ugly ones.

One incident ensured that whatever I felt personally, I would become persona non grata with the miners of North East England. Thatcher had appointed a hard-as-nails industrialist called Ian MacGregor to restructure the coal mining business across the country. He came to visit a pit at Ellington in Northumberland not long before the strike began. Tempers were high, to put it mildly. Reporters from newspapers, TV, and radio gathered en masse to witness his reception. Inevitably, it was a highly hostile one. He was walking with mine officials when a line of strikers brushed past the few police on duty and bore down on him. As the first of them barged into MacGregor, he fell to the ground. His eyes rolled shut. He appeared to be in a dead faint. Confident my cameraman was capturing the scene, I darted forwards, and with a man from the *Daily Mail*, hoisted Macgregor up. On his feet, he looked around, dazed.

Whether the *Mail* man and I had intervened or not the miners could easily have trampled MacGregor. They wanted to. And probably get some kicks in at the hated media at the same time. They did not, I think, because for a few seconds, they were shocked at what they had achieved, seeing Margaret Thatcher's loyal servant sprawled out. They paused long enough for policemen to push them back. It made a juicy story, especially with great pictures of the incident. More especially so with the BBC reporter, on camera, right in the thick of it all. The striking miners loathed me for it. The episode did me no professional harm when it appeared on the main bulletins. MacGregor and I were destined to meet again, in circumstances even more bizarre, if less chaotic.

Industrial turmoil was only part of the daily work. Not since my local paper days had I covered such a range of stories. The area from Northumberland down past the Tyne, the Wear and the Tees has always produced plenty of hard news. There were fatal house fires, some serious road smashes, and all the other bits and pieces of human misfortune which, if it suits you, make reporting such a stimulating job. Murders happened regularly. I sat in court and watched as three dishevelled men were paraded in the dock. They had set out on an armed robbery and ended up being accused of murdering a policeman in County Durham. If they had more than a few bruises on their faces, that seemed perfectly normal. *Life On Mars* has been a recent and enjoyable piece of TV entertainment inspired by the way policing used to be. Pretty close to the truth it was.

Sometimes a commission would come from the features side of the BBC. I was asked to investigate highly dubious money-lending practices on Tyneside. You met some real villains doing that. My camera crew loitered outside a nasty individual's house while I was locked inside having a disagreeable conversation with a notorious character. My crew heard most of it because I was 'miked up', wearing a small microphone linked to a pocket-sized radio transmitter. They caught the conversation up to the point where my highly reluctant interviewee ripped the microphone off my jacket and hurled it on the floor. It made good television. As the pictures showed the exterior of a house mostly in darkness, the sound track was of me asking about the ludicrous interest rates charged and unpleasant threats made to those who could not pay up. A lot of cursing meant a lot of bleeping out. And the conversation ended with the mike being silenced. I escaped a beating up. Narrowly.

Another out-of-the ordinary assignment had me sent off to Southampton. I reported live from the dockside, clutching a microphone and being deafened by cheering crowds welcoming troops back from victory in the Falklands. Slightly battered, the cruise liner *Canberra* nosed its way up Southampton Water. I had imagined I would never see British servicemen return from a foreign war in my lifetime.

In those days, the Corporation's news system relied on energetic local reporters much more than it does now. Newcastle was always reliable for the first hint of winter snow. TV Centre in London would ask us to film some in our area. Hop north up the A68, and at the Scottish border, at remote and windswept Carter Bar, you could rely on some white stuff long before it hit most places in the UK. I was eager to get pieces on to the main BBC1 bulletins, and not only to impress London. Reporters like Tony Baker and I were paid by the story. Indeed, if any item went over the magic three minute mark, the fee went up. It encouraged freelance activity at an intense level.

So there was a direct correlation between how much you did and how much you pocketed. The freelance attitude has stayed with me ever since. 'Don't work, don't eat' is how I have always summed it up. A competition developed to see who could actually make the most money in a day, compiling as many reports as possible for as many outlets as would take them. Tony Baker was the winner, allegedly sleeping in the office to keep his fee-earning hours up. The advent of the BBC's *Breakfast News* was a good opportunity for me. I would ring the police and the fire brigade in the earliest of early hours and write up several stories based on their information. Each I would be paid for. Finally, I would go in the studio and read the regional inserts into the main *Breakfast* show. And guess what: there was another fee for presenting the regional bulletin. I must add that such systems, which certainly encouraged high productivity, have long been swept away by an increasingly cost-conscious BBC.

Not all the stories were dark ones. There were events like the sheep auctions at the beautiful village of Rothbury. Sometimes I was sent over the Pennines to talk to people in Cumbria, then served by the BBC from Newcastle. It was hard to believe I was at work when I drove along the east-west A69 and took in some of Britain's grandest scenery.

I learned some tricks. Our base was in a curious old building that had been what used to be called a 'lying in' hospital. A maternity unit would be its modern equivalent. One quiet afternoon, a man walked down the still vaguely medical-like corridors to give a recorded interview. It would be about a book he had written. He was sitting in the studio, while the book telling of his exploits climbing some fierce far-away mountains lay forgotten in someone's in-tray. It was found, thrust at me, and I was told to go and do the interview. It was a big book and there was no time to read it. If confronted with such a problem, try this. Pick any of the later pages and a find a line that is a bit out of the ordinary. Maybe it's '. . . the first thing I do when I get back to camp is call my mother . . .' As you sit down to put your interviewee at ease say: 'I was fascinated that you are so careful to call your mum . . .' The interviewee will be eating out of your hand. You can bluff through thereafter. After all, surely you must have *read* the fascinating book to pick up such a trifle.

Sometimes not having time to do your homework could land you in a dither. I set off to interview a man I was sure was famous as a veteran undersea explorer. When the crew and I found quite a young man sitting at a piano, it was a panicky few moments before I established that I was to interview Jacques Brel rather than Jacques Cousteau.

Another feature for network television was about the dream of a car factory being built on Wearside, to create lots of jobs to fill the gaps as traditional industries withered. The opening sequence had a car appearing, headlights on, through a typical North East mist – a sea 'fret' they call them – on the runway of an airport in Sunderland. I got out of the car and opened the documentary on the lines of 'One day, it's hoped they'll be making cars here . . .' It seemed rather far-fetched. But Nissan of Japan did come to Wearside, and one of the most successful car plants in the world arose where a few small planes once came and went.

Now and then, something inconsequentially jolly turned up that could I could sell to the main BBC bulletins. A piece about a body builder in Newcastle who exploded huge glass jars by blowing into them made a nice tailpiece for the then *Nine O'Clock News*. A certain John Humphrys was the presenter. As my report finished, there was Humphrys actually chuckling. You don't very often see that.

Back in the studio I observed a master at his work. The *Look North* presenter was Mike Neville, one of those top-class performers whose names may not be much known on the national stage, but whose skills make them a household name in their backyard. Mike had started out as an actor. He was the perfect, cool-headed performer to present a news show where, often, careful plans went awry. I think he enjoyed the screw-ups the most. I am sure the viewers did. I always say Mike Neville never taught me anything. I learned so much of the essentials of this peculiar job just by observing him. To hold it together when the programme is falling apart. To cope with the 'talkback' in your ear, the instructions from the control room. To listen to them and talk at the same time. So many times I am asked: how do you do that? I always answer that if you can't – you're in the wrong job.

We all learn from mistakes. On live television, mistakes are very public. For one *Look North* show, I sat alongside Mike Neville to introduce, and do live commentary over, several film sequences about an industrial dispute. All had been done in a rush. The films had to be laced together in one reel on a machine that would transmit the pictures when cued. Once laced up, you could not play around with the order. I was too hasty writing the script and selecting the sequence of the pictures. On transmission they and the commentary did not match up. I would begin introducing one scene for another to pop up. It was my own fault. As I floundered, the studio camera cut back to Neville. 'Sorry about that,' he announced smoothly. 'It's been a busy day . . .'

Afterwards the station manager swept into the newsroom where I sat sorrowing over my incompetence. 'That was the worst thing I've ever seen on British television,' he barked. My viewers treated me better. Geordies are naturally friendly. As I walked through Newcastle the next day, a kindly man said: 'You had a bit of trouble last night . . .' Even the manager's harsh words did not seem quite so cutting a little later. Another programme suffered another embarrassing cock-up. This time not mine. The show over, the manager stormed in, cross again. 'That,' he said, 'was the worst thing I've ever seen on British television.'

Gradually I got more confident. One task was to do a short regional bulletin put out late on Saturday evenings. It was produced with just two staff. There would be one technician lurking around to ensure the whole apparatus was functioning. In the studio, a presenter had to listen in his or her earpiece to a countdown from London telling them when to start. A button on the desk had to be pressed to get on air. You had to read the scripts, fumble carefully for other buttons to reveal then cancel slides to illustrate the items, and press yet another button to finish on time as London counted you out. Most important, before the start, you had to remember to put the powerful studio lamps on. A fellow presenter forgot one night and the whole bulletin was read by a spectral figure bobbing about in the gloom.

It is hard to overstate Mike Neville's colossal following in the North of England. It would stay with him when, after I moved away, he switched across from the BBC to the local ITV company, Tyne Tees. First-hand experience of just what a god he was came when I got married for the second time. Brenda Firth was a reporter on the Newcastle *Evening Chronicle*. Before we met, a mutual acquaintance – Dianne Nelmes, a fellow *Look North* reporter who would go on to be a senior figure in ITV – talked about a girl she knew: 'You should meet Brenda. She's divorced, and got two kids, just like you.' I thought that was actually *not* my notion of a good idea.

Yet when we did meet, at the BBC club where lots of local journalists gathered at the end of the working day, I was transfixed. In December 1983, in the unprepossessing surroundings of the Gateshead register office, she became my wife. The registrar lady obviously thought she knew me from somewhere, although she could not quite place me. This often happens if you are on the TV. 'Do you shoot in Norfolk?' a lawyer fellow once asked me in London. He seemed suspicious when I denied it.

The Gateshead registrar managed to overcome her curiosity to get on with the business. Her formal demeanour evaporated when my Best Man walked in. The registrar could hardly speak. 'It's ... it's ... Mike ... Neville!' she started. The civil ceremony went rather sluggishly, with the registrar flicking her eyes back and forth from the Great Man to the marrying couple. Sometimes, she faltered over some of the crucial words. I have sometimes wondered whether I was legally married at all. Or perhaps I was married to Mike Neville.

Brenda and I began house-hunting in the towns to the west of Newcastle. Compared to the South East, you could get an awful lot of property for your money in Corbridge or Hexham. As we searched we both knew I was restless after two years on Tyneside, and that I wanted to be back in London. That was partly because every fortnight I would dash southwards after Friday evening's *Look North* to open up a house in Surrey, to spend a precious weekend with my two children. Sunday night I would race north again. I came to know every curve and bump on the A1.

Brenda's two children were Justine and her young brother Daniel. Justine, then nine, was understandably uneasy about life changing with the marriage. Her father was an architect with offices in Newcastle. He lived in a village close to Brenda's home at Ryton in the Tyne Valley. Don't worry, I told Justine, things will go on just the same. Quite wrong. The North East, with its enchanting people both at the studios and everywhere else, had taught me so much and brought me the greatest possible personal happiness. A telephone call from an old *Financial Times* colleague would, however, change all our lives a great deal.

Wedding day: friend Maggie Gibbons, me, Brenda, Mike Neville. Who was I married to?

THIRTEEN

Channel Four came along to challenge BBC1, BBC2 and ITV – and in the pre-digital age they were the only substantial channels – in 1982. We stood around in the BBC's Newcastle newsroom, watching the first show. It was *Countdown*, hosted by Richard Whiteley. Only that mid-afternoon quiz programme and Channel Four News survive from the original schedule. The news slot, at seven o'clock, was designed deliberately to break away from the usual pattern of TV news output. The brains at Channel Four decided they wanted fewer insufficiently explained pictures, and more analysis. Not an easy remit.

Independent Television News (ITN), famous for *News At Ten* with the bongs in its title sequence and often sharper reporting and presenting than the BBC, was chosen to produce Channel Four's bulletin. ITN went mostly to the classier end of the national newspaper market to find the programme's executives and some of its journalists. After a couple of years, the combination of inexperienced performers and often worthy stories stodgily told left ratings seriously down.

Channel Four warned ITN that it had only a few months to get audiences up, or lose the contract. The editor, who went on to publish some very successful reference books, was let go. ITN put in one of its young production stars, Stewart Purvis. Channel Four wanted to keep the distinctive feel. Pieces should still be as rigorous as possible, but done by people who understood TV. Sir Richard Attenborough was Channel Four chairman. In his inimitable way, 'Dickie' Attenborough explained to Purvis what was needed: 'Remember it's all show business, darling.'

The political editor was the very capable Elinor Goodman, who had been at the *Financial Times* with me in the 1970s. It was she who called me at home on Tyneside, saying the search was on to find someone to do the business stories. Someone who understood finance and economics, and who could also 'do telly'. Down I went to London, to discuss the future with one of the best television news executives of all time,

David Nicholas, eventually to become Sir David. He was ITN's editor-in-chief. His enthusiasm and his vision of what the station could do with Channel Four News were infectious. Like the thoroughbred Welshman he was, Nicholas was a great talker. So much so that I had to break in to remind him that I had to get back to Heathrow and catch a plane for Newcastle. The god Mike Neville had broken his leg, and I was fronting *Look North*. David Nicholas swept me out of the building and into a taxi. I could hardly believe it. ITN, held in such high regard inside and outside television news, had offered me a job.

It was only after I had left ITN, two decades later, that Stewart Purvis, who rescued Four News with his hard-driving and occasionally ruthless leadership, confided to me that ITN had been horribly close to losing the contract. If it had, I might have been looking for work again in very short order. Instead, there were thrilling years helping to shape a news programme which has established the highest of reputations. In 1984, it was all to be done.

We were encouraged to experiment, while trying not to fall into the dullness that had lost the initial audience. Having been with the BBC when the miners' strike began, I joined ITN as the battle between Arthur

New boy at Channel Four News. Mid 1980s. (Picture by ITN)

Scargill and the miners on one side and the Coal Board under the gruff Ian MacGregor on the other reached its climax. As they slung insults and accusations at each other, Purvis had the bright idea of getting them together to debate the issues in front of Channel Four viewers. The pugnacious Scargill was keen; the cautious and uncharismatic Mac-Gregor less so.

Because I had been reporting the dispute extensively – to say nothing of rescuing MacGregor from the enraged pitmen of Ellington – Purvis took me along to the Board HQ near Hyde Park Corner to persuade the chairman to take part. I sat across from him and his PR chief, wondering what all the thumping I could hear was about. It was MacGregor, kicking the table crossly at each idea for the confrontation he did not like. He did not like much. Eventually, we returned to ITN, pretty convinced that the Coal Board would not 'put up'. It wasn't long before the news was due on air. At Purvis's command, I started scrambling together a story of the day's developments in the strike to fill the expected hole at the top of the programme. Very shortly before seven o'clock, word came from Board headquarters. MacGregor would, after all, debate publicly.

It was the sort of coup that built Purvis's reputation, and rightly. He could be fiercely critical. His eye for detail and quality was formidable. At the end of a show, he would often come scowling into the newsroom, determined to nail why some error or other had got on to the screen. 'Post mortems on the living' I called his nerve-wracking inquests.

C4N, as the programme was called internally, did not have a big staff in its early years, and no permanent correspondents abroad. Which meant that the United States, the source of so much that matters the world over, was not properly covered. We did have a producer based in Washington, although that did not get the story count up much. One of Purvis's answers was to send me off to the States for a fortnight to find stories.

It was a rare opportunity then, and unheard-of in today's budget-conscious conditions. I criss-crossed North America, interviewing business types in Manhattan, computer wizards in the West, car giants in Detroit, and go-ahead retailers in the Blue Ridge Mountains. The Blue Ridge tale required the impromptu hiring of a small plane from a bumpy little airstrip on the edge of a sleepy town whose name I have long forgotten. I have not forgotten that as we gained height, the pilot announced his suspicion that we might have lost the nose wheel on take-off. I tried not to think too much about that as we flew and filmed a vast new shopping mall in the mountains before coming into land at another less-than-pristine airfield. The nose wheel, it turned out, was undamaged.

The joy of simply being told to go and find things to report on was that I could visit places I had always wanted to, and then fit stories around them. There was a respectable if not spectacular gold rush going on in northern California It meant travelling to San Francisco, where I was booked into the swanky St Francis Hotel. Present-day budgets, again, would rule out such a luxury berth. I arrived at the hotel to meet my local freelance camera crew. Our discussion was brief. They had been ordered to Washington. Political developments needed covering and there was a shortage of crews. They tossed me the keys of a hired Lincoln Continental parked in the hotel basement. It would be two days before another crew was available. Off I went in the Lincoln, dodging round the famous cable cars on the steep hills that dot the city. I crossed the Golden Gate Bridge for a very enjoyable tour of the Napa Valley and its vineyards. Work soon required doing again. The gold mine we visited obliged us by setting off a blast louder, closer, and more dangerous than we had been expecting. Channel Four News was lucky not to lose a correspondent and his crew as fragments of rock came crashing down around them.

Next, we went just outside San Francisco to the university campus at Berkeley. One of America's most celebrated economists, Milton Fried-man, had gone there after making his name as one of the right-wing theorists at the 'Chicago School'. Margaret Thatcher was a fan. He spoke her political language. Lots of other people were very unimpressed. Whatever your own views, he was a fascinating person to interview. First, the crew and I took a few shots around the university, to set the scene of academic endeavour. The cameraman found it understandably difficult not to point his viewfinder at the hordes of attractive female students who ambled around the sunny campus. It is too long ago to recall what wisdom Friedman had to dispense. I do remember what he told me when asked what it was like to fetch up in California. 'It rots your brains,' smiled the grand economist. He did not seem too fussed by that. He died at the age of 94 in 2006, still in San Francisco.

One practical consideration no-one in London had thought to warn me about was how to get my filmed material back into the UK. I strode up to Customs with a bag full of videotapes. The customs officer was aghast. 'You can't just bring those in,' he said. Why not? 'Well . . . they could be pornographic films.' I invited him to start looking through the 20 or so tapes. He waved me into Britain, with a reminder about the need, if there was a next time, to fill up all the requisite import forms.

Reporting for C4N was hard graft, especially as I had the Business and Economics brief. It was always a challenge to make decent television out of subjects often puzzling even to an audience willing to think as well as watch. It was a regular test of both basic journalism – finding a real story in what was going on – and making the best use of the medium's opportunities. How do you start a report on an economic summit in Toronto? I could not resist a shot of a Canadian security man peering down an open manhole, checking whether anyone wanted to blow up the world's top finance ministers. The idea was to hook the viewer with the first few seconds of picture. The television equivalent of the all-important first paragraph of a newspaper piece.

Sometimes I strayed from the Business beat. My great interest in trains made me the choice to report on the horrific Clapham Junction railway accident. Three trains collided in the morning rush hour. Thirty-five people were killed, five hundred injured. We had a camera position on the top floor of a pub looking right over the scene. Amid the shattered coaches were some awful sights. An overworked technician working on re-signalling had let two wires touch that should not have done. The

TV's so glamorous. A chilly day, reporting the Channel Tunnel breakthrough, 1990.

death and destruction were hard to comprehend. There was another viewpoint, a bridge straddling the tracks. Camera crews were lined up along it, shoulder to shoulder. It made the point that television had come to rule the news world when the stories were dramatic and the pictures graphic.

The Channel Four show was anchored in the main by Peter Sissons, who had a formidable reputation as a forensically-inclined interviewer. Others deputised on occasions. One Thursday evening after the programme finished, editor Purvis approached me. 'Peter's not in tomorrow. You'll be presenting. Ok?' I was delighted, and nervous. Not long down from a regional newsroom, I was surrounded by some of the brightest and best in television news. I decided to consult the big man.

Sissons was lolling. His feet were thrust up on the desk in front of him and his eyes were half-closed. Fifty or so minutes of live TV could be wearying, even for a seasoned presenter. I explained to him who would be inadequately filling his seat on the Friday. Did he have any tips? 'Get yourself a cup,' he said, swinging his feet down. Puzzled, I fetched one of those plastic things that sit alongside water coolers everywhere. Sissons opened the bottom drawer of his desk, produced a bottle of whisky, and poured me a large one. 'Drink up,' he commanded.

Between glugs, I said: 'Thank you, Peter. But . . . what has this to do with presenting Channel Four News?'

'Oh. Just don't do that *before* the programme . . .'

It was his only advice. To host Channel Four News was a fantastic yet often frightening way to make a living. Particularly with the demon-eyed Stewart Purvis ready to take apart your performance. One evening that old Tory bruiser Norman Tebbit ran rings round me. I knew it. Purvis's strictures were well taken. I must have been getting it right most of the time because I was allowed to continue.

People are often bewildered to learn that no-one trains you to 'read the news'. On C4N you did much more than just read, and that has become true for almost all TV newscasters now. Once news bulletins were the preserves of actors. Over the years, good journalism came to be the main requirement. You must have what Sir David Nicholas, my first ITN boss, called 'a well-stocked mind'. The only test of whether you are up to the mark – and whether the viewers take to you – is to do the job a few times. It is a competitive jungle and its laws can be heart-breaking.

The pitfalls are not entirely to do with how you introduce a programme and the stories being carried, or how you tackle those slippery politicians. There are other traps. In the mid 1980s, C4N would finish with a 'top shot', taken from a camera high up in the studio. Once the presenter had said Goodbye, the director would switch to the top camera. The viewer would look down on the anchor shuffling his scripts, and chatting quietly – remember microphones might be still on – with whoever might be left sitting alongside. Over the shot, the credits would be run. This was the roll call of those who had helped put the show on. Many of the job titles meant nothing to me. And quite a few of the names I had never heard of.

As the titles unfurled, I *thought* I heard the studio director say in my earpiece that I was no longer in vision, that they had switched away from me. Even by Channel Four standards, it had been a long and demanding programme. A major event was rattling along in the background. An aircraft was being hijacked somewhere in the Middle East. A journalist called Trevor McDonald was among the correspondents who had come into the studio to keep us updated on the developing story. I had felt the strain, and thinking I was safely away from viewers' gaze, I buried my head in my hands. If it had been a cartoon sequence, the last bubble would have read: 'Phew!'

The catch was ... I was still *in* vision. A million or so punters witnessed my exhaustion. As I left the studio for the newsroom, the humiliating truth dawned. The worse thing about such a balls-up is not the folly itself but the way kind colleagues try to dismiss it. 'It wasn't so bad,' someone said. Yes, it was. 'No-one would have noticed.' Yes, they would. Purvis was less encouraging. Something from him about 'What on earth were you thinking?' The very worst was still to come. As I sat in the editor's office, clutching another plastic cupful of whisky, a producer stuck his head round the door: 'Nick, your Mum's on the phone. She wants to know if you are all right.' Floor, open. Swallow.

C4N tried nightly to be thoughtful and probing as well as watchable. On the other side of ITN they put out the more brash bulletins for ITV. I began working for both departments, sometimes reporting for one, sometimes presenting for the other. No other ITN journalist did that, and it took some juggling. A significant break came for me in 1990, when I was due to read the Lunchtime News for ITV. Margaret Thatcher's grip on the leadership of the Conservatives had been on the wane for a while. Her resignation when it came was still a great shock. It appeared as a flash from the news agencies just before 9.30 in the morning. I headed straight into the studio. ITN went 'Open Ended', taking over the airwaves with no definite finishing time. Nowadays, news rolls on endlessly, Britain's best exponents being the BBC and Sky News. In 1990 it was most unusual.

For me, it was tremendous experience and exposure, handling interview after interview in the studio and 'down the line' with politicians and pundits in front of cameras all over the place. At midday, I got a short break, and was amazed to find myself replaced, temporarily, by Alistair Burnet, then ITN's most senior presenter. I was back for the extended Lunchtime News. A day of high drama ended with me switching back to reporting and doing the final item for *News At Ten*, an attempt to sum up Mrs Thatcher's premiership. The vital opening shot was carefully chosen – the leader triumphant at a Tory conference in her early years – and so were the words. I was proud of them: 'She who once could do no wrong . . . the darling of her party.' The last shot was a perfect discovery quarried from the ITN archive of Margaret and her husband Denis sitting quietly together on a park bench. For them, it was to be retirement, though not as most of us would know it.

If there were dramas aplenty outside the ITN building, there was a major one inside. The BBC poached Sissons. A dim view was taken of such defections and he was told to quit ITN without delay. The editorship of Channel Four News had been taken over by Richard Tait, a former senior BBC executive who would later return to the Corporation and sit on the BBC Trust. He summoned me in as the news of Sissons's departure spread. I would be replacing him, at least for a while. It was a good moment to remind my boss of one of the basic laws of economics: when the supply is short, the price goes up. I got my first Newscaster's contract from ITN, with a gratifying rise in salary.

Are TV presenters paid too much? Some for sure. On the news side, the rewards at the top are very good, though mostly defensible. A bit like your airline pilot, we are not paid well to guide a smooth programme along. We get the money for knowing what to do when it all goes wrong. In the Press I had worked for some top-class and inspirational people. To cope with television's bumps and grinds, I could not have had better professionals to emulate than Mike Neville in the North East, and Sissons himself at ITN.

The stint in the chair at Channel Four News came as a serious international conflict exploded. Saddam Hussein invaded Kuwait and the world watched as diplomacy gradually failed and war loomed. Quite a few Britons were in Iraq when the crisis began, and they became

Back to his roots: A special guest when my first paper, the Surrey Mirror, *moved to a new office. 1994.* (Picture by *Surrey Mirror*)

Saddam's enforced 'guests,' as he liked to call them. They were hostages, and they included one frightened little boy. Pictures of him with the Iraqi dictator came in as C4N was on air, with the Foreign Secretary, Douglas Hurd, beside me as a studio guest. We ran the pictures of the boy and I asked for his immediate reactions. His face showed he was truly horrified.

The war to throw Saddam out of Kuwait was upon us when I opened a morning newspaper – one of my old ones, the *Daily Telegraph* – to read that Channel Four News was to have a new anchor man. If my breakfast was a bit spoiled, Jon Snow had a glittering CV, even though he had not immediately shone when asked to stand in as a Presenter. It is often the case with great reporters. That did not deter Channel Four from seeing him as their future star, which he has proved to be over two decades. He quickly learned the tricks of holding a programme together, and Snow made the 7 o'clock slot unthinkable without him.

I was bruised to find out that I was to be ousted by reading it in the paper. I have always made it a policy not to get upset over the ups and downs of who-gets-what and why-do-they-not-want me. Even so, I was unimpressed when told that I had not been forewarned because there was a worry about news leaking out. Charming. Having said that, I knew that in the long term C4N was not for me.

There was one important job still to do for the outfit that had shaken off thoroughly the early description of being 'Channel Bore'. As George Bush Senior and John Major assembled a coalition of forces to liberate Kuwait, Richard Tait offered me a new show. He explained it would go out at midnight, run for two hours, use interesting guests, and bring in live reports of the fighting. The transmission timing sounded dire. Don't worry, said Tait, people will watch. He was right. The first programme was very nearly a disaster. The man appointed to mastermind it came from ITN's Westminster studio, and was unfamiliar with the way we put news together at HQ. He found it impossible to get any scripts printed out and handed round, or to get any words put on my autocue. Another tiresome obstacle was to discover with minutes to go that we were not starting at midnight. Channel Four's idiosyncratic schedule meant we would begin at ten to 12. A scramble to get in front of the cameras, and an awful lot of unscripted ad-libbing, got us underway.

The Midnight Specials worked far better than I had imagined. Guests ranged from senior military figures to politicians of all sorts, plus wild cards like authors and opinionated newspaper columnists. Refereeing was best, I found, if I always confessed straight away if something was happening about which I had no clue. Students of TV history may know that the first rolling news channel, CNN, originated in Atlanta way back in 1982. Few if any other broadcasters had thought it worth following its example. The First Gulf War made CNN's reputation. We would frequently cut to pictures from the channel which was beaming stuff out from the Middle East war almost all the time. I say 'almost' because once when I was tipped off that interesting CNN pictures were coming in, we switched away from our studio just too late. For a few seconds, I tried to explain why we were showing a white horse cantering across the screen. We had hit a CNN commercial break.

There were moments of real tension. I had a high-ranking RAF man beside me when we took live pictures from Israel where air raid sirens were wailing to warn of incoming Iraqi Scud missiles. You had to wonder what was in the warheads. And how Israel, a nuclear-armed state, might react. I noticed my RAF guest had gone very white. Saddam's Scuds turned out to be mostly a nuisance. The Israelis got American help to mount effective anti-missile defences.

CNN had a 'good war'. By the time George Bush Junior and Tony Blair decided to invade Iraq early in the next century, they had plenty of rivals. Midnight Special-type shows had become two-a-penny. In 1990, our pioneering got us noticed. *The Guardian*, reviewing TV coverage of the Kuwait crisis, said watching our shows was like being invited to listen in on a well-informed dinner party. Gratifying praise. But my mind was made up to leave the C4N team and go full time over to the ITV department, where the audiences were bigger if not always so discriminating. Even though I was still within the bosom of ITN, Four News organised a leaving party. In the video made to mark my farewell – always among the most superior productions in TV newsrooms – one old *Financial Times* mate appeared up to tell tales of my newspaper days. He recalled that I would set off to talk to tycoons not with a smart briefcase but with a plastic shopping bag. He reckoned it was a good way to make an interviewee think I would be a soft, unprepared interviewer.

Rather than plastic bags, camera crews with all their gear accompanied me when I reported for the shorter ITV bulletins. Lord Beaverbrook, the Canadian-born businessman who harried and bullied his staff into making the *Daily Express* a great newspaper in its heyday, knew how he wanted stories told. They should be 'light and bright, tight and right.' Exactly the ITV formula. And there were new colleagues to get to know. Among them was the newscaster Carol Barnes, who became a great friend. Life was to be savagely unkind to her. She lost her daughter Clare

Remembering a lovely friend: my mum Diana and Brenda, naming a Brighton bus after the much-missed Carol Barnes. (Picture by *The Argus*, Brighton)

in a skydiving accident in Australia in 2004. 'Barnesy' herself died of a stroke, to the great distress of those who knew her, four years later. She lived in Brighton, not far from my mother. Diana was there when I named a bus after Carol, an honour that seaside city accords its most distinguished residents.

Back in the mid 1990s, for me another dip and swerve on the rollercoaster was coming. Three years after switching to the workaday scramble of ITV from the high-minded ways of Channel Four, the man in charge of ITV coverage, David Mannion, wanted to see me. 'Nick,' he said, 'we need a new Royal Correspondent.'

FOURTEEN

I agreed with the boss. We certainly needed better Royal coverage. It dawned a bit slowly what he was suggesting. 'You don't mean me?' I said. He did. Rather a surprising job offer to someone who has always had a strong feeling that the monarchy is an anachronism.

He waved away such objections. A decent reporter was required. Any other questions? Very few pieces of career advice are really useful. Here is one: if someone asks you to take on some big responsibility, seize the moment to request something in return. The pleasantly-sized pay rise on the abrupt departure of Peter Sissons was a good example. It was time for another. 'Can I go on the trips?' The answer was Yes. In the 1990s, prominent Royals tended to pay visits abroad much more than they do now. I was in for some serious globe-trotting.

First, though, how to find out about this strange institution that whatever clever-dicks like me may think continues to command such public loyalty? I decided to tackle it two ways. First I would wine and dine a former Royal Correspondent. Always best to get the well-informed yet properly circumspect outsider's view first. After that, I would try the same entertainment route with some Royal insiders. Ronald Allison was doubly useful. He had been a distinguished reporter on Royal matters for the BBC, before spending several years behind Palace walls as the Queen's Press Secretary. His word portraits of members of the Family were terrifically useful. As we left the restaurant, he had one more important tip: 'Keep a diary.'

Time to lunch the insiders. Prince Charles's charming Press Secretary revealed happily that he always stood in his master's presence, and always exited backwards after any consultation. Charles came over a stickler for protocol that was not observed so strictly at headquarters, Buckingham Palace itself. A phone call to the courteous lady on the Palace switchboard had me put through without trouble to the Queen's Private Secretary, Sir Robert Fellowes. Would Her Majesty's most important employee join me for lunch? I expected a polite but firm refusal. I was wrong. He would be delighted. Where? The Caprice is a classy place only a few minutes' walk from the Palace, tucked just down the road from the Ritz Hotel. Over the Caprice table it was useful to show the Private Secretary that ITN's new Royal Correspondent was a reasonably genial type, a hack with good table manners. My guest became distracted. A prominent actor was among the other diners. Sir Robert was fascinated. 'Isn't that . . .?' he whispered. You might have thought someone doing his job would be hard to impress. Celebrities were beginning to dominate everyone's life.

And celebrities did not come more celebrated than Diana, Princess of Wales. A dozen years before, I had wandered among the crowds near St Paul's, taking some time away from my subbing shift at the *Financial Times* to marvel at the enormous numbers who wanted to see the newly-married Royal couple. By the time of my lunch at the Caprice, and my early enquiries into the bizarre world of the Royals, that marriage was coming apart. Much of the detail of just how bad things were between Diana and Prince Charles had still to come out. The media was beginning to learn, and beginning to be manipulated by one camp or another. Another lunch, another senior Royal official. This one pursed his lips as we were finishing our meal, and asked: 'Have you heard of . . . bulimia?' So my Royal reporting days were to be dominated by two kinds of story. The dark side, the focus of such intense fascination, would be the travails of the beautiful young Princess. Her unhappy life and ghastly death would be the biggest stories I would ever cover.

Apart from getting caught up in a riot or two – and witnessing someone firing shots at Prince Charles – happier times were generally had with the sights, sounds and sensations of Royal visits abroad. Few assignments could have covered more countries. There is a nice little game to play when I talk to audiences about my adventures with the Royals. 'Who here has been to, well, Bhutan? Or the Falklands? Or . . .?'

Bhutan – have *you* been there? – was simply amazing. To get there involved travelling from Khatmandu in Nepal. Just a chosen few – one reporter from the BBC, one from ITN, one cameraman, and a news agency man – skimmed past the Himalayas in an executive jet. Everyone rushed to the left-hand side windows to see Everest, unclouded, brooding, and dark, as we headed for the long airstrip outside Bhutan's capital, Thimpu. The runway was long because the thin air meant planes needed plenty of room to land in, and take off from, the tiny kingdom high in the mountains.

Only in later years did the King of Bhutan allow his subjects to have television. It was one of several out-of-this-world restrictions which made the place so fascinating. Only a very limited number of foreigners were allowed in. This combination of a TV ban and unfamiliarity with outsiders had an immediate and alarming impact on my work. We got off the small plane to find ourselves in the middle of a tournament featuring the national sport. It is archery, and no-one seemed to either notice or mind where we quickly set up the gear so that I could do a piece to the camera. What a wonderful location. Buddhist temples on the hillsides, prayer flags slapping in the wind, and archers traipsing around in Bhutanese versions of the kilt, their national dress.

Trouble was, the kilted archers were a hundred or so yards to one side of us, and their targets a hundred or so yards to the other side. They carried on firing arrows right over our heads. I thought it would be prudent to film elsewhere. Chris Squires, an ITN cameraman who had courageously ducked and dived his way through danger in innumerable battles and riots, wearily plucked a cigarette from his lips. He looked round the camera at his cowardly reporter. 'They know what they're doing. Just get on with it!' I now have some inkling what it would have been like to be at the battle of Agincourt. The arrows sounded as though they were ripping through thick cloth as they sliced through the air. More actually dangerous for us were the twisting mountain roads of Bhutan. They were mostly narrow bumpy tracks where meeting anyone else on a blind bend left you with a choice between a rock face on one side and a sheer drop on the other. Wrecked trucks littered the valleys hundreds of feet below. Other traffic consisted largely of Indian army vehicles, on patrol in what has been the fought-over and still tense area between India and China.

Royal tours could be insubstantial cavalcades of superior types bowing and scraping as the exalted visitor made small talk hundreds of times over with complete strangers. That could be dreary, and no-one back in London would be interested. Sometimes, though, where the Royal visitor went could make the story. Prince Charles loved to walk, and he loved to paint. After we had woken, short of breath in our freezing chalet accommodation in a Bhutanese valley – desperately cold until the sun appeared for a few boiling hours – we were taken to the foot of a mountain that he would be climbing. He would get some peace at the top to set up his easel and capture some of the most entrancing scenery anywhere on Earth.

Ropes and crampons were not needed. But it was a very stiff bit of uphill walking. We few reporters went ahead of him. A shot of the intrepid ITN correspondent would be included. Chris Squires, cigarette still in place, set up his gear at a turn in the stony path. As I puffed up and past him, I said something like: 'I don't know how the Prince is getting on, but this certainly is one arduous climb.' As I plodded on, Squires called out: 'Great. Just need to do it once more, Nicky. Get the shot slightly better.' Back down the wretched hill I went, turned, and paced back up, uttering the words again.

Further on, we stopped again and waited for Charles himself. He was probably glad of an excuse to take a breather. So often abrasive in his dealings with reporters, he talked away happily. All of us were awed by the surroundings. A place to bring his young sons one day, I wondered? Absolutely, he said. That was the glory of Royal tours. Observing the usual formality and protocol when you are thousands of feet up a Himalayan peak would have seemed daft.

One question which so often comes up is, what were your favourite moments? I have no doubt. The year was 1995. South Africa had renounced apartheid, Nelson Mandela was out of jail, and the country had been allowed back into the Commonwealth. The Queen visited. It was a week or two inside a highly-coloured, exciting kaleidoscope. Walking along a road near a township in Port Elizabeth, I heard chanting getting gradually louder behind me. Mandela, with an unofficial escort singing their way along beside his slow-moving car, was coming my way. He was standing up in the back, acknowledging the huge enthusiasm among the waiting crowds. I climbed up on to a small embankment which brought me to eye level with him. As his car crept past, he turned towards me. 'Good Morning, Mr President.' 'Good morning.' He smiled, his head dipping as we looked at one another.

In the township, the stunning rhythms of black African music and dance were bewitching. Getting back to Port Elizabeth itself with our video was going to be difficult, as there was only one narrow dirt road out of the township. As the Queen's convoy swept past, my cameraman and I leapt into our hired car, and joined the back of the stream of fast-moving vehicles. The one in front of us had some large, heavily-armed detectives, who gazed suspiciously at us as we kept up with the convoy, racing through clouds of dust and finally through the deserted streets of Port Elizabeth, other traffic banished and traffic lights zipped through at red.

It was sheer boys' own adventure. The very best was yet to come. The Royal Yacht *Britannia* had sailed out to South Africa. Not carrying the Queen and the Duke of Edinburgh, mind. The Labour government who sanctioned her building in the lean years after World War Two insisted on an economical design, and modern stabilisers were not included. The Queen flew to and from the UK. But *Britannia* was ideal for receptions, and one was organised for the afternoon of a very important day in Capetown.

For me, the day had begun with going to a service at Capetown cathedral. Archbishop Desmond Tutu, that sparkling apostle of majority rule, gave the sermon. His voice breaking so often into a chuckle, he swept his congregation along with his talk of the 'rainbow nation' and the way seismic change had come so peacefully. Thanks largely, of course, to the charisma of people like Mandela and Tutu himself. Next stop was the Parliament, to be addressed by Queen Elizabeth. In front of her, old enemies sat by side. Big fleshy Afrikaaners, who had been persuaded to give up power, alongside members of the ANC, regarded as terrorists in apartheid days. There were men and women in swirlingly colourful clothes from tribes across South Africa. Many of the MPs listening to the Queen would either have been locked up – like Nelson Mandela – or be in hiding when I had last been in their country.

Copies of big speeches like that are usually handed round in advance. It gives broadcasters a chance to make sure they record the key points. We were warned there might be an extra line, not in the prepared text, right at the end of her speech. The Queen glanced at her script, looked up at her audience, and closed with the words of the anthem beloved of those who had struggled for freedom: 'Nkosi, sikelel' iAfrika!' God, Bless Africa. The applause thundered out. The tears had come in every eye. Tough, seen-it-all reporters were not exempt.

After that was a reception on board *Britannia*, to which I had been invited. It was a glorious African afternoon. Not a whisper of wind, the sky Royal Blue (of course), Table Mountain to one side, the berth from which Mandela had been taken to long imprisonment on Robben Island on the other. For a few minutes, I stood on the deck – and chatted with the Queen. We talked of the almost unbelievable assembly she had addressed in the Parliament. 'Wonderful' was a word she used. It was the only adequate one. During our conversation, my mind wandered ever so slightly. Enough for me to think: 'Not bad for a lad with five O levels . . .'

One of the curiosities of Royal visits was that so often they brought reporters face to face not just with the best of a country, but also the worst. In South Africa, the poverty in the township of Soweto, Mandela's base, was rather worse than I had remembered. Promised reforms were failing to help the millions of blacks at the bottom of the prosperity ladder.

Perhaps the hardest sights, and smells, to get over were in that cripplingly overcrowded state, Bangladesh. The Prince of Wales went to show his support for British charities trying to help unfortunates like those who erect pitiful, flimsy homes on the embankments built to defend the capital Dhaka from the ever-present threat of devastating floods. Families literally cling to life on the steep slopes. Regularly they are either washed downwards by heavy rains, or flooded out as waters rise with great suddenness.

To give my crew a chance to reconnoitre the place, the ITN team had arrived one evening ahead of the Prince and his party. I was driven into the heart of Dhaka in a mini bus. Street lights were non-existent, and the roads were crowded with pedestrians and quite a few poor souls stretched out and apparently dying in the gutters. All that plus every imaginable form of transport. The most worrying were heavily-laden lorries that came lurching towards us, very often completely on the wrong side of the road. They were trying, as we were, to avoid the many cavernous potholes that took some spotting in the gloom. As well as the lorries there were overloaded buses, other erratically-driven cars, hordes of bicycles, and many large animals moving in all sorts of unpredictable directions. Bangladesh was originally part of the British empire. After yet another close call with a rickety truck, my driver – his eyes thankfully glued to the road ahead – said to me: 'It's all the fault of you British!' Really? How did he figure that? 'Everything was much better before you left.'

Back at the glitzy end of the Royal world, the yacht *Britannia* did not have much longer to sail around. Tony Blair's Labour Government, knowing the old girl had to go, declined either to finance a replacement or even discuss a joint deal with private investors. Early on a misty morning I was on a launch which put out from Gravesend pier on the Thames, the sort of dank riverside location that would be a perfect backdrop for a Dickens novel. The launch was taking a small party of journalists alongside *Britannia* for her final run up the Thames. It was sensible not to look down at the mud-coloured water as we clambered up a tiny ladder to get aboard. The effort was worth it to be able to be on the bridge of *Britannia* as fireworks and cannon went off passing Greenwich, and under the spans of Tower Bridge rising like a triumphal arch to let the yacht pass into the Pool of London. It was a poignant farewell for a vessel that had brought much prestige for Britain when she was seen abroad.

The last time I saw her on 'active service' was during a visit by Prince Charles to Kuwait. *Britannia* was on station earning its keep, as so often, with the hosting of receptions on board to encourage trade links with the UK. Wheeling and dealing over, she set off towards her final duty, the handover of Hong Kong to the Chinese. A lone piper stood on the Kuwait dockside and played a haunting lament. Cue a few more tears as we saw that potent symbol of Royal power sail off to the East on a blisteringly hot evening.

The piper had been playing 'Highland Cathedral'. Some years later I was asked to speak to a party of Americans who, after golf at St Andrews, had dinner on board the yacht, now in retirement and dry dock in Leith. The visitors were agog to think they were enjoying their evening where the Queen of England and her companions had once entertained. They were even more impressed to think that several Royal honeymooning couples travelled on *Britannia*, including Charles and Diana. As the meal got under way and I prepared to tell a few Royal stories, a piper was playing away on the dockside. I requested that his repertoire should include 'Highland Cathedral'. Back came a message:

'Mr Owen. The Pipe Major says it refers not to Scotland but to *Cologne* cathedral.'

I smiled. 'Please tell the Pipe Major to play it anyway.'

Most Royal tours went smoothly and to the sort of rigid timetables that fussy Palace types insist on. They must have approved mightily of Thailand, whose monarch, King Bhumipol, was so revered that to say anything critical could easily land you in jail. In a country palace in the jungle near the Cambodian border, it was flabbergasting to see elderly ladies of the Thai court approach their king on their knees. And withdraw from his presence backward, still on all fours. Britain's Royals must have wondered how long it had been since anyone had done that back home.

FIFTEEN

Some Royal visits went badly. Things got very strained when the Queen travelled first to Pakistan, then to India. Not many mortals could jet between the two great rivals, and it was a tour where the diplomatic eggshells were extremely thin. Everything went sour just before we left Pakistan. A shame, because it was an interesting trip, especially accompanying Prince Philip around the Hindu Kush and along the dusty border with Afghanistan, not an expedition that could be done easily nowadays. Trouble came in the capital, Islamabad, when the Queen addressed Pakistani MPs. Her speech had some words about hoping to see a settlement of the bloody unrest in Kashmir, where Pakistan and India blamed each other for the incessant instability. It sounded – slightly – as though Britain sympathised rather more with Pakistan's position.

Once we had flown across the tense border between the two countries, the reception in India was tepid. Anyone less than the Queen would have been unwelcome altogether. The Royal media pack duly reported the political tiffs, to the growing fury of the Royal entourage. A Royal Press Secretary bellowed angrily at me during another reception, this one in the dreamy beauty of Kerala in the south of India. He made it sound as though I was single-handedly wrecking the Royal show.

Hardly any foreigner visits India without going to the Taj Mahal. A great spectacle which is beaten, to my mind, by the Golden Temple in Amritsar, the holiest of shrines for Sikhs worldwide. The temple glistens blue and white as well as gold, a vision whose astonishing beauty makes it hard to be remember the terrible upheavals Amritsar has seen. One notorious historical incident soured relations with Britain and the bitterness has lingered ever since. In the middle of the city, troops under the command of the British General Dyer emerged through an alleyway and opened fire on a crowd of unarmed civilians in 1919. Prince Philip's duties included unveiling a plaque to the victims. The numbers killed and wounded have long been disputed, and the Duke grunted his scepticism

112

at the total number of those said to have suffered. He said he had served in the Navy during the war with Dyer's son, and he knew the figures were exaggerated. A point of view, although it was hardly the time or the place to express it. More big stories on British TV and in the papers. More rows with Royal advisers.

Another run-in with the Duke of Edinburgh came on a journey round Switzerland. He was President of the Worldwide Fund for Nature, based in Geneva. His Palace advisers thought that it would be good for him to be seen visiting the Fund's headquarters and going on to promote the good cause among wealthy supporters. I am afraid journalists are always on the lookout for mischief. Hadn't the Queen's loyal husband, in earlier, less sensitive days, been on tiger shoots in places like India? A look through the archives confirmed it.

The plan was to interview Prince Philip near the end of his Swiss peregrinations, to sum up his visit. Even in his 70s, the Prince kept to a very lively schedule, and the only opportunity to hear from him was, rather bizarrely, on a train journey. We got two camera crews aboard, one to film him, the other to record me asking questions and listening to answers. This was luxury. Usually, 'on the road' – or even on the rare occasions when filming on the rails – one camera is used. After the questioning finishes, the single camera is turned on the reporter. Some questions might be recorded, and some 'noddies' are shot, where the interviewer is seen listening attentively to his subject. If the process is lamely done it can look ropey in the final edit.

With two cameras rolling, I asked the Prince if, having shot tigers, he now viewed wildlife preservation differently. It was understandable that it was no longer a seemly pursuit for Royal celebrities. I expected he would talk of attitudes changing, and everyone needing to think of the plight of wild beasts. It was he who turned wild. The eyebrows knitted sharply, and a flash of temper came.

'I only ever shot one,' he croaked angrily. 'And I don't what you know about it. I don't expect you were even born at the time.' My riposte, caught on the second camera, was delivered calmly: 'I'm afraid I was, sir ...' The exchange was carried prominently on the day's bulletins. Rage exploded at Buckingham Palace. It would be a long time before any further favoured access was allowed to ITN, and particularly its cheeky Royal Correspondent.

Switzerland was a pleasurable excursion. Often, Royal visits involved exhausting scrambles in and out of often uncomfortable hotels, and on and off planes that were rarely luxurious. There were exceptions. I envy the Royal Family nothing except their transport arrangements. Occasionally we would get a lift home on the Royal Flight. Luggage would be collected early on departure day by a baggage master. We would be whisked on to the plane just ahead of the Royal party, and the aircraft would be up and away without delay. On its designated Purple Flight Path, the Royal plane gets priority. Sometimes the smooth routine is interrupted. I happened to be on the flight deck chatting to British Airways' most senior pilot as we flew high one night over Iran. When Tehran air traffic control called up the aircraft, they got its call sign slightly wrong. Not very reassuring. And weren't the Iranians very hostile to the UK? Was it possible that a missile could be on its way to take out the Royal flight? Oh, no worries, said the BA captain as he gently corrected the voice from Tehran. The Iranians were fine and very professional. Who isn't fine, I wondered? Oh, in his view, the French. Rather unreliable. Now that could bother you, if you thought about how many UK flights flew out and back over France every day.

There were no more in-flight hiccups, and as usual the Queen's Flight swept undelayed into Heathrow and stopped by the VIP area. The Queen, Philip, and assorted retainers were down the steps and away smartly. The media picked our luggage off the tarmac where it had been dumped. Cars were ready to take us straight past security and passport control. No anxious waiting for bags to come off any carousel. Within minutes I was left outside Terminal Four, calling my wife for a lift home.

It was not only diplomatic upsets that could turn a Royal tour into more than just applying words to pretty pictures. Those who planned the Prince of Wales's visit to South America in 1999 had a tricky itinerary to get right. It started in Argentina, whose continuing irritation over ownership of the Falklands persisted even 17 years after losing the war with Britain over the islands. Political differences were put aside and the Prince was received politely everywhere. The Argentine capital is one of the most pleasant cities on earth. They do dance the tango in the streets, and the polo ground where the Prince indulged his favourite sport was almost too serenely English to be true.

The mood after dark on the streets of Buenos Aires was different. A mob angry that a Royal from the old enemy was in town charged through the streets one evening. Several petrol bombs were thrown. One exploded a few feet from me. The police replied with tear gas. As the protestors retreated, reporters and cameras chased after them, with a good deal of spluttering and coughing on all sides. And it was not just regular police officers who went in to deal with the trouble. Very threatening and very burly men with long batons appeared out of the shadows and were not too particular who they struck out at.

The disputed Falklands were the Prince's destination. A direct flight by the Royal plane was out of the question. We had to go via sleepy Uruguay and its capital Montevideo. There was not nearly so much to commend the place as charming Buenos Aires. However, its beach – with the wreckage of the scuttled Second World War German battleship the *Graf Spee* a few hundred yards offshore – is a spectacular one. Always a believer that colleagues back in London should feel some envy when one was in an exotic spot, I made sure we recorded a piece to the camera on the sweeping shoreline.

From Montevideo it was a couple of hours' flying on the Prince's new British Airways Boeing to take us to Mount Pleasant, the military headquarters in the Falklands. Nick Witchell of the BBC and I got ourselves off the plane quickly and rode in a Chinook helicopter the last few miles to the capital, Stanley. If the Royal Flight had been extremely comfortable, the Chinook was quite the opposite as it spluttered and shuddered low over the bare grassland of the main island. It was worth the discomfort for the exhilarating reception in Stanley, where crowds surged forward, welcoming us as the advance party for the really important visitor. Charles was the most senior Royal to go to the islands since the 1982 conflict. The graves of British servicemen at Bluff Cove and the simple, even slightly scruffy, memorial to those who perished on HMS *Sheffield* have to be among the most powerful reminders of one of the series of wars that Britain has fought since World War Two.

The 1982 war may have been long over but reminders of it were everywhere. Just outside Port Stanley, on the single main road that runs to the Mount Pleasant military base, was one of the many minefields still littering the islands. Falkland children followed the British curriculum at school with one important extra lesson. They were taught how to spot and beware of the mines. Serious attempts to clear them only started early in 2010.

Hazards when reporting from strange places come in all sorts of guises. In 1999, most of the roads on the islands were dirt tracks. Reporters would be given lifts during Prince Charles's visit by helpful local volunteers. I set off with one of them in his Japanese-built four-wheel drive to get some urgent pictures back to Stanley from some remote spot in the west of the Falklands. We were speeding along a dirt road high on an embankment when my chauffeur lost control. The four by four swept round broadside, careered on for a couple of hundred yards, and finally plunged backwards down a steep bank. Once the two of us had agreed we had not actually broken any bones, and I tried not to dwell on the many mines that had been sown alongside the highway, the impressive tractive power of the people carrier let us clamber back up on to the road and on our way.

The Falklands could be eerie as well as dangerous. As I walked along the shoreline one evening I was intrigued by a thin, intense line of white light on the horizon. The Falklands' economy depends heavily on fishing. Huge lamps are hung over the side of trawlers to attract squid in great numbers. In the stygian black of the South Atlantic, the pools of powerful light are said to be one of the few sights on Earth visible from way out in space.

Globetrotting for TV can be a bizarre as well as exhausting way to make a living. I nearly missed out on a huge story, as well as almost earning more air miles quicker than anyone in history, when I went to Australia at the start of another of Prince Charles's tours. The producer who met me at Sydney airport looked worried. There was a suggestion I might have to turn straight round and return home. They were short of a presenter back in London. That job took priority because I was contracted to be a newscaster. I always said ITN got the Royal reporting thrown in for nothing. Somehow, the hole in the presenters' rota was filled and I got on with covering a long if not especially promising Royal visit. Many Australians were ambivalent, at the very least, to the idea of being subservient to the British monarchy. And earnest old Charles was only Her Maj's son after all. By this stage, his marriage to Princess Diana had fallen apart and she was not with him. If she had been . . . now that would have been a different matter.

Lack of interest in Charles changed abruptly after an evening of the highest drama in a Sydney park. The Prince was on a stage, about to present some schoolchildren with prizes. Duty compelled a bored ITN correspondent and his cameraman to be present. A police band behind Charles played, over and over again it seemed to us, the wearingly familiar 'Waltzing Matilda'.

Most of the audience were seated on the grass. A few yards from me, a man sprang up. He was brandishing a gun. A couple of shots rang out as he sprinted towards the Prince. Chatting with the Queen on the deck of *Britannia* had given me time to relish all the details of a big moment. Now, the slow-moving part of my brain that night in Sydney had me wishing devoutly I would *not* witness the assassination of the Prince of Wales. The police band seemed oblivious and carried on playing. It was left to the Premier of New South Wales to apply his old rugby-playing skills and wrestle the gunman to the floor. My cameraman and I sprinted forward. I saw the pistol clattering around as arms and feet thrashed around on the stage. More slow-motion thinking had me hoping the gun didn't go off again, especially when it was pointing at me.

And the Prince? He did what he so often did, and still does. He fingered a cufflink and gazed with a puzzled frown at the melee around him. His sang froid endeared him to Australia. And we had a heck of a story. A little later I stood in another park in Sydney, ready to talk to the camera, the framing to include the famous Opera House just in case any half-asleep viewer didn't register where we were. That is television news for you.

All the headlines and most of the *News at Ten* programme would be taken up with the one story. I would be leading the show. Before we went on air, presenter Trevor McDonald and I chatted via my earpiece. What's the weather like in London, I enquired innocently. Pouring with rain, said McDonald. I glanced up at the cloudless Sydney sky and considered for the umpteenth time what a lucky hack I was.

We criss-crossed Australia after the shooting incident. The crowds were much bigger than originally anticipated. 'Good old Charlie,' they called out everywhere. The gun turned out to be a starting pistol. The man who fired it, putting a terrific scare into those guarding the Prince, was protesting about the treatment by the Australian authorities of refugees fleeing by boat from Cambodia. He was charged with threatening unlawful violence and got 500 hours' community service. His name was David Kang, who ten years later qualified in Sydney as a barrister. He said he had been deeply depressed and expected to be gunned down by the police before he got close to Charles. He added that he had 'moved on' in his life after what had been 'an extremely traumatic experience.' Not just for you, Mr Kang.

If Charles could show stoicism in face of apparently great danger, it was probably a trait he inherited from his grandmother. The Queen Mother was until her death a reliable star turn for Royal reporters. Her birthdays – born in 1900 she could not avoid the appellation of being 'as

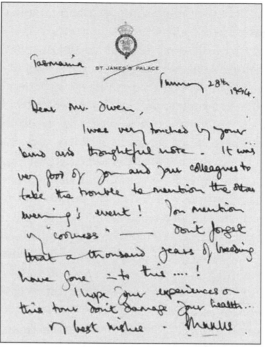

Princely thanks: a letter from Charles after the shooting during his Australia tour.

old as the century' – always drew a big crowd, and always got big coverage. She did not give interviews. It was said that just before her marriage to the Prince who would become, unwillingly, King George VI, she did tell a reporter about her wedding preparations. Her frosty father-in-law, George V, sternly disapproved, and the order went out to ban the Press from ever having close contact with her.

No sound engineer picked up the conversation I had with her at Prince Charles's 50th birthday party, thrown for him in Buckingham Palace. I have always thought it extraordinary that any journalists were invited in that night. Could we be trusted to behave? The Queen was introducing her mother to some of the guests, and spotted me in the crowd. 'Now, you know who this is,' the Queen said as they advanced on me. I had been told by Ronald Allison in that briefing lunch before starting out as a Royal Correspondent that I must not assume, in spite of pleasantries, that the Queen Mother would ever actually *like* me. With that in mind, what do you talk about with the woman who for the lifetimes of every person in Britain had to be the very embodiment of Royalty? 'What's it like, Ma'am,' I said, 'to have a grandson of 50?' The old lady turned half away from me. 'I don't think of him as 50,' she said, putting a hand out

118

and downwards. 'I think of him as he was when he was very small, when he was ... little Charles.'

There were so many stories about the Queen Mother. About her fondness for gin and Dubonnet, her passion for horseracing, for blithely ignoring the Royal Family's ancestry and saying how deeply she distrusted the Germans. The Luftwaffe had, after all, bombed Buckingham Palace when she and the King were inside. The best tale was told to me by the late Peter Ustinov, that raconteur extraordinary, who swore he witnessed and heard an exchange between the Queen Mother and William, later Lord, Rees Mogg, a former editor of *The Times*. He had been appointed to head some broadcasting regulatory body. He was very tall, the Queen Mother very short. She was so short, in fact, that almost everyone who met her had to bow a bit whether they wanted to or not. 'Sir William,' she said, gazing up in her stately way at the giant who embodied 'the great and the good'. Did his new job, she asked, mean he was in charge of 'keeping naughty things off the screen until after nine o'clock?' Bending his head well down to reply, Rees Mogg agreed it was so, while wondering uneasily where this chat might be leading. 'Pity,' came the reply. 'A bit late for me.'

She was teasing. The Queen Mother was famous for staying up late. Often later than weary courtiers could cope with. I may not have been a monarchist, and she probably would not have liked me, as Ronald Allison had advised. Yet I was very sorry when she was no longer around to give us good, and cheerful, Royal stories.

My last assignment as Royal Correspondent took me to Northern Ireland. The 'peace process' and the dawn of power-sharing in the province meant the Royal Ulster Constabulary was to be renamed the Police Service of Northern Ireland. The RUC had suffered grievous losses in the struggle against Republican and Loyalist terrorists. On a drizzly morning in a field in Belfast, the Queen presented the RUC with a collective George Cross, saluting the bravery of so many policemen and women since the Troubles started in 1969. It was intensely moving to watch as she met several officers severely disabled in the line of duty. Only once before had the George Cross gone to a group rather than an individual. It had been given to the island of Malta in recognition of its valiant defence against the Germans in the Second World War.

For the evening bulletins, the RUC let me handle the Medal, to show it close up to the ITN camera. As usual, the Queen kept to herself what she really thought of her Royal constabulary losing its old identity to adapt to changing times.

SIXTEEN

Being face to face with the person who you could argue had the most famous one in the world was an odd experience. As a Royal reporter I had seen Diana, Princess of Wales, many times. Yet she was usually some way off, surrounded by crowds. The adulation she attracted came to be derided by some commentators after her death. In life, she had a way of upsetting cynical preconceptions.

If I wasn't being asked about the Queen, the question was usually: 'Have you met the Princess . . . what is she *really* like?' I got a fair inkling when we sat side by side for lunch, when we talked of all sorts of things. Most especially, we talked about television. ITN had managed to persuade Diana, by now apart from Prince Charles, to come to our headquarters in London's Grays Inn Road to meet some top TV people. And me. Stewart Purvis, my old Channel Four News boss who was by now editor in chief, explained that I would be sitting next to her. 'She'll want to talk to you,' he said. 'She's fascinated by anyone on television.' It was another 'Robert Fellowes at The Caprice' moment. You might imagine someone who merely made appearances on TV news pro-grammes would be beneath the radar of a Royal Princess, especially one exposed to so much media attention.

It was a strange encounter for a number of reasons. Word spread quickly that she was in the ITN building, so reporters and cameras from our rivals turned up at the front door. Diana got in unnoticed. Anxious ITN executives soon started fretting about how she could be smuggled out. That was amusing for a Correspondent who spent a good deal of time arguing with Royal officials who wanted to stop *me* setting up a camera where they did not want one.

I was late for the big lunch. I had a good excuse. Editors and chief executives could dance attendance on an honoured guest at any time. I had to read the Lunchtime news bulletin first. Once finished, I took the lift up through the sleek, airy, HQ to the directors' dining room one floor above the noisy newsroom. The building was designed by the renowned Norman Foster, an architect who is big on grey and blue. Go to Stansted Airport's terminal and you will see the same general colour scheme.

The ITN site had strong journalistic roots. Two Hundred Grays Inn Road was previously home to the *Sunday Times*. ITN was then in Wells Street, close to the BBC's Broadcasting House. I had gone from there one day to Grays Inn Road to pick up Andrew Neil, then editor of the *Sunday Times*, and film him in his chauffeur-driven car going through the gates of News International's new, more or less union-free plant at Wapping, in Docklands. Great was the rage of the soon-to-be-redundant print workers, who hurled insults and threats as we drove into the Wapping complex. Great too was the rage of Neil's employer, Rupert Murdoch, when he spotted a TV crew and reporter within the gates. For several subsequent nights, I witnessed the blazingly angry protests as lorries loaded with News International titles sped out from the new print works. The scenes were rather worse than those during the miners' strike. The police did remarkably little to prevent pickets going under the wheels of the speeding trucks. It was amazing no-one was seriously injured.

Once the old *Sunday Times* place was redeveloped into the new ITN base, the Queen came to declare the new building open. ITN staff were lined up to greet her. How amusing it was to see hacks who professed little time for such flummery wear their best bibs and tuckers, and smile away in the hope of catching a word with their monarch. I was given a specific assignment. I sat at a desk from which short summary bulletins were normally delivered. My task was to outline to our visitor just what 'reading the news' entailed. As if she hadn't heard it before. When the Queen walked up, I swivelled round in my chair and gave a brief explanation. It occurred to me that I was the only person in the whole of ITN to be speaking to her while sitting down. Having been reminded by a flunkey to rhyme the word with 'jam', I explained: 'Ma'am, I'm sorry not to get up. But I'm attached to the desk by wires from the microphone and my earpiece. If I get up, I'll pull the whole bloody lot over.' The Queen broke into a broad smile, and laughed.

It was a couple of years later – unhappy years for a Royal Family where divorce was becoming as common as among their subjects at large – when the Queen's daughter-in-law came to lunch. It is justified, I think, to describe Diana as the world's most famous person because who else

Making the Queen laugh. With ITV News editor David Mannion. (Picture by ITN)

would be recognised anywhere where there is mass communication? A decade after her tragic end, magazine publishers in need of a sales fillip were still finding excuses to put her picture on their front covers. When I walked into the room beside the main dining area, she was facing me, leaning back slightly against a drinks table. She was on mineral water. I never saw her touch any alcohol. The all-male company was enthralled, and conversation was slow.

Until we sat down. As my editor in chief Stewart Purvis had predicted, she soon chattered about television, about what she enjoyed and what she did not. Asked about the way she was treated in the Press and elsewhere, she seemed to have developed the sensible Royal habit of not paying too much attention to what was written about her. And television news tended not to get embroiled in the more unpleasant stories, so we clucked sympathetically when complaints were made about media harassment. The truth was that we got beaten to scoops by newspapers who got more inside stories than we did. Rival Royal factions preferred to connive with the printed media. It was obvious Diana herself deliberately cultivated certain sympathetic newspaper journalists in her 'war' with Buckingham Palace.

The lunch was early in the year. Suddenly the Princess turned to me with an unexpected question: 'Do you know what was the most popular programme on television on Christmas Day?' I could not resist. 'Well, ma'am. It wasn't your mother-in-law's broadcast.' She chuckled. 'I know,' she went on. 'It was the edition of *Eastenders* on Christmas afternoon.' Interesting information. The relevance, though? Diana waited a moment or two, until she had the whole table's attention. 'I watched it at Kensington Palace. On my own.' It was the saddest of insights into how her marriage – picked over so endlessly in public – had brought desperate unhappiness. She was alone on Christmas Day because the rest of the family, including her sons William and Harry, were with the other Royals for the usual Christmas break at Sandringham in Norfolk.

The ITN lunch over, Princess Diana was hurried out down back stairs and into an underground car park, so she could escape one more day of the media's compulsion to follow her every move. My work often involved waiting around as she paid her official visits. Her popularity was unrivalled. One day, as I hovered on a pavement outside a hospital, a woman stopped me and said: 'You are so lucky.'

'I am? Why?'

'Because wherever you go, everyone is always smiling.'

She meant of course that everyone was smiling because the Princess was around. The lady got the mood absolutely right. And if Diana was a star in Britain, she was a whole constellation when she went to America. In New York, as she got out of her car to go into a dinner in a smart hotel, a huge crowd roared out: 'Di-an-A! Di-an-A!' In the world of celebrity she shone the brightest. At a ball organised in her honour in Chicago, everyone who was anyone in American politics, the movies, and the business world packed in and strained to catch a glimpse. My cameraman and I whipped off our shoes, and struggled to keep our balance on top of an expensive-looking, highly polished, slippery table to get a good clear shot as she swept down a curving staircase picked out in a spotlight. No Hollywood celebrity could have matched the dazzle. When she finally got to sit down, guests wandered past the table, gazing upon this icon as she ate her dinner. It was as if a mediaeval sovereign had appeared in their midst.

If Diana had suggested becoming Queen of the USA I reckon the job would have been hers. There were rumours that after her marriage breakdown she was thinking of going to live in America. Not true. She told me herself she knew the constant attention there would be even more trying than anything at home.

A much more low-key event came in the August of 1997. One evening the Princess of Wales was the principal guest at a show at the Tate Gallery, beside the Thames in London. ITN 'had the rota', meaning we would be the crew to film this unexceptional Royal duty, and make the pictures available to the BBC, Sky News, and any other broadcasters who wanted them. Diana came in, smiled briefly at me as she clocked the camera, and moved past to shake more hands and make more small talk. I noticed how broad her shoulders were. She was spending a lot of time in the gym. Newly-divorced people often do.

The Tate event turned out to be her last formal engagement. It would be the last time I saw her. She went off on the holiday with Dodi Fayed that was to end in their deaths in a Paris road tunnel. I was on holiday myself, though at home, when an old friend and senior ITN colleague, Robin Elias, rang to tell me about the accident. I was in the studio in the early hours when the word came that the Princess had died. The week that followed was my biggest story.

I still think they were some of the saddest few days in modern British history. Those big on hindsight like to blame 'the media' for somehow whipping up an inappropriate frenzy. Untrue. I was not alone among reporters in finding the dark mood of the huge crowds that converged on London perplexing. It was a daily exercise to keep coverage accurate and in proportion, to avoid anything that could count as rabble-rousing. Walking along The Mall close to Buckingham Palace, seeing and hearing the murmuring of discontent, I saw why senior police officers worried that Charles might have a bad time of it at his ex-wife's funeral.

A couple of ITV network programmes followed. The one I was proud of set out to chronicle that strange week between the crash and the funeral. Very few holidays were booked. People did not want to talk about buying or selling houses. Less happy was a documentary investigating the talk of conspiracies that had caused the death of a Princess. Dodi Fayed's father Mohammed, shattered by grief, spent vast amounts of time and money trying to prove murder had been committed. I never believed any of it, although there were mysteries in who did what and why that dreadful night in Paris. Trailers for the programme – intent on whetting audience appetites – played up the whispers and rumours. Few commentators who later lashed ITV for its treatment of the subject bothered to listen properly to my carefully-written conclusions. Some serious and legitimate questions hung in the air, even if a tragic accident and a drunk driver were to blame. It didn't save me from being described as 'a knave but not a fool' in one national newspaper.

In the corner of a restaurant in a Swiss ski resort there came a surprising postscript to the days of Diana. The Prince of Wales liked to go late in the winter season to ski in his favourite spot, Klosters. Reporters would follow, and we would be allowed limited filming of him on the slopes at the beginning of his week away. The Princes William and Harry became enthusiastic skiers. A couple of years after their mother died, I was in Klosters for the annual skiing story. We set up our editing gear in the corner of a jolly little restaurant, and started putting together a piece for the news bulletins. The young Princes had a new Press secretary, a vivacious black woman called Colleen Harris. She asked if the boys could come and watch the editing process. I declined, knowing that having them around would be bound to delay our work and attract much distracting interest from diners in the restaurant. We agreed the boys could come to see the final product, and I would explain how we had put it together, and why we had chosen certain sequences.

Chatting with their mother in the ITN executive dining room had been an experience. It was almost matched by having her two sons looking over my shoulder, and joshing one another as they heard the bits of their recorded voices that I had chosen to include. They talk of the 'politeness of kings'. Like Diana – and indeed Prince Charles – they called me 'Mr Owen', the way I have hardly ever been addressed since my time on the *Surrey Mirror*, back in the more staid 1960s. My main impression was that their shy courtesy showed how like their mother they had both become. I thought so again in the spring of 2011, when William married Kate Middleton. It is a union that has set off a whole new wave of interest in the Royals. Any taste for republicanism in either my children's or my grandchildren's lifetimes would seem to have been banished.

Relations with William's father were often fractious in the six years I was Royal Correspondent. More than once Prince Charles had snapped angrily at me, his face red with annoyance. It happened once in Klosters. The irrepressible Tara Palmer Tomkinson, a friend of the Prince, was putting some ski gear into a Range Rover and stopped me to have a chat. He appeared, and thundered: 'What are *you* doing here?' Even the heir to the throne could be told that there was nothing wrong in standing and talking in a public car park.

One scoop I did get, leaving the newspapers floundering in our wake, was the discovery that Charles would be admitting to adultery in a television interview with Jonathan Dimbleby. The story and the reactions it provoked led *News at Ten* for two or three days before the programme itself was shown. I became increasingly nervous that the key passage would be 'pulled' from the final version. Surely that would mean instant dismissal. In all the years since my local newspaper days that has always been a fear in the back of my mind. The old unease about being found out. The interview was duly aired as we had forecast.

I gave up reporting the endlessly curious ways of the Royals in 2000. Several years later I was very happy to become a so-called 'ambassador' for the Prince's Trust, Charles's organisation that offers help and encouragement to young people who have had difficult starts in life. It's a role that brings some treats. My wife and I were invited one autumn to have a look at Prince Charles's marvellous garden at Highgrove. A heavily scented shrub caught my interest. Asked what it was, one of the gardeners climbed down from the apple tree she was pruning, and snipped off a cutting for me.

A little later, I was in conversation with the Master of Highgrove himself. The cutting was in my button hole. I explained hastily that it

A visit to Prince Charles's Highgrove garden, with actor Martin Clunes and Brenda.
(Picture by Paul Burns)

was not me who had cut it. I did pass on his gardener's sensational information. The shrub concerned was reputed to be a reliable aphrodisiac. No irritated princely face this time. Instead, good-natured laughter all round. If the Prince of Wales had sometimes hated what I was up to, and what ITN said about him in my days on the Royal beat, we seemed to have been forgiven.

SEVENTEEN

Lying flat out as I was wheeled towards the operating theatre I had one preoccupation. 'Right one . . . right one!' The surgeon walking alongside grinned. I was not to worry. A line had been drawn round where his knife, or its modern equivalent, would cut into me. You do wonder in such circumstances whether you will wake up again. And in my case, whether I would be in a position to work again, at least at the old pace.

I may have left the Royal pageant behind, but reading and reporting all sorts of news kept me at full stretch. A habit of being on holiday for really big stories had persisted. Brenda and I were on the Italian island of Ischia when we walked past a shop where television pictures had drawn a crowd. I wondered why a New York fire engine was driving around covered in ash. Only later did we sit on the edge of our hotel bed and learn from BBC World what had happened to the Twin Towers in New York, the Pentagon in Washington, and the fourth hi-jacked airliner brought down by the courageous response of some of its passengers. We managed to bag the last two seats on a plane leaving Naples for London, where I reported on the packed church services, the dazed crowds around the American embassy, and the deep shock everywhere as the details of the events in America unfolded. I was on air a lot. Other senior ITN correspondents twiddled their thumbs in extreme frustration for several days because the US would not allow them to fly from the UK to the States.

Four weeks after the horror of 9/11 I went to New York – on Concorde. The supersonic plane had been withdrawn from service after the catastrophic accident near Paris when an Air France Concorde had picked up debris on the runway as it roared into the air, and came down a flaming wreck to kill everyone aboard. I had reported live from close to the crash site. A few fields in outer suburban Paris were littered with blobs of twisted wreckage. Many assumed the Concorde would never fly again. Modifications were made so that the fuel tanks would be less

128

vulnerable – a stray chunk of metal that had fallen from a preceding take-off had done the fatal damage – and an inaugural flight was laid on from London to New York. There was only space for a handful of journalists. Three and a half hours after Heathrow we were on the tarmac at JFK airport. Mayor Rudolph Giuliani came aboard to greet us to his beleaguered city. 'Welcome to New York,' he drawled. 'Spend your money!'

Ground Zero, where the Twin Towers had been destroyed, was still smouldering and stinking of death and shattered skyscrapers. A helicopter ride over Manhattan gave a grandstand, stomach-churning view of the site. At street level, Ground Zero was an almost unbearable vision of the ultimate terrorist hell. The photographs and pleas for help finding missing people, which were strung on every available railing round about, were pitiful. The cataclysm of 9/11 did powerful harm to the finances of the airlines, and supersonic flights became a luxury British Airways and Air France could no longer afford. Concorde had little time left.

The following summer, my wife grew tired of hearing about my 'grumbling gut', an annoying and persistent irritation in my intestines. She persuaded me to go to a specialist. Eoghan Owen is no relation, but he saved my life. After a thorough examination, he reckoned I seemed quite fit. He is a strong believer in prevention, so he thought at 55 a scan would be a sensible idea. In a truck in the car park of a local hospital, I began to learn the worst. As he studied a series of images of my insides the radiographer was obviously concerned about something. I pressed him to tell me what it was. He said he really should only pass on information to the relevant surgeon. As we walked across the car park back to the main building, he relented. 'You've got a tumour on your right kidney . . .'

Kidney cancer is classed as rare. The raw figures account for the rating, scant comfort to those who find themselves with the eighth most common form of the disease. Caught in time, the outlook can be very good. If the tumour is encapsulated, hidden away in the kidney, prompt removal of the organ is the best form of treatment. If the cancer has spread, the outlook is not so good. All this I was to learn in the days that followed my operation. After my friendly radiographer had broken the bad news, Brenda and I sat in front of the next and most important medical man, the engaging Mel Jennings. He would do the operation to get my right kidney out. He was the first to use the most dreaded of words. It came almost as an afterthought as we discussed what needed doing. 'Now, we never promise a cure from cancer . . .' The reaction was like a laborious double-take in a B movie Could he be talking about . . . me?

The journalist in me fired off questions. I had no symptoms – blood in the urine is the one danger signal, and my troublesome guts were irrelevant – so how long had the tumour been there? How long might it have been before it was diagnosed if there had been no scan? Would it then have been too late, and fatal? Kidney cancer has many puzzles, and there are few answers. Jennings was anxious to get me into the operating theatre. Did I have a few days' grace? He agreed, if a bit reluctantly. I wanted to grab a few days' holiday with our great friends Alan and Margaret Gibbons, three hundred miles away in the enchanting wilds of Weardale, close to the very top of the Pennines. Brenda thought I was mad. Before we set off to the north of England, I sat in the garden of our Surrey home and bawled my eyes out.

The tears were emphatically not for myself. Others who learn that their life is no longer to be taken for granted often recount feelings that I identified with completely. Nature has a way of wrapping you up, of cocooning you. The anguish comes for those close to you. Their suffering is the hardest thing to bear. Even so, I did cry. I sat in my garden on a sunny afternoon and wept because of the memories, suddenly so sharp, that came back from more than 20 years earlier. They were of my father in his last illness.

My Dad retired from Rothschilds bank when he was 60. His health went downhill soon after, and pancreatic cancer was diagnosed. He had several operations. After one of them, I visited my parents at their home in Brighton to find my father frail and in distress. 'Cancer' was never mentioned. It was obvious he was in considerable pain. He seemed so vulnerable. As I faced my own crisis, I thought of him old and sick, of how he had lost my mother, and what he had endured during wartime in the Navy. I realised how little I really knew him. I wished I had told him how much I had missed him when I went to boarding school. And I wished above all that I could have been more of a comfort in his last few months.

My worry about getting the right-hand kidney out was because of a sad recent case in Wales where a patient had the wrong one removed. Jennings did his work, and after a week in the hospital – where most evenings he would sit in my room and discuss the shortcomings of the health service and the politicians who paid such lip service to it – I returned home for two months' recovery. It was a nice summer, and there were times I felt a fraud.

Just after the operation, I had the unsettling experience of reading my own obituary. Well, it was almost my obituary. ITN had published a Press release revealing that I had been operated on for cancer, and that I was making a splendid recovery. It was a pre-emptive strike. I knew that many weeks away from the screen would be bound to get the Press interested eventually, and it was a good idea to get an accurate version of events out quickly. The papers treated me very well. I was amused that my old employer, the *Daily Telegraph*, talked of me being 'rushed to hospital'. There had been no blue lights, and anyway there had been the week away in Weardale. Not much of a rush. Then there was the *Mirror*, and a long article across the top of an inside page. The story started accurately with the ITN press release before a description of my meandering 'career'. It ended with words about 'married . . . two children . . . two stepchildren . . .' It did sound awfully like my obituary, with a bit of re-writing here and there to cater for the fact that I was still 'right side of the grass' as a chum once put it.

Cancer charities came calling, hoping I would help in the endless quest for funds. Often it has involved auctioneering, a new skill to be acquired, and with it the pleasure of discovering just how generous people can be. I always explain that I am up on my feet for purely selfish reasons. I have every reason to support the immensely important work being done to find out more about kidney cancer. Some of the best brains in medicine are involved. For them, for their patients, and for myself, I gladly bang as many drums as anyone cares to wheel past me.

There is increasing use of keyhole surgery, and maybe my right kidney could be dealt with now without leaving the long silvery scar that stretches across the front of my stomach. It is hard to spot, though, and that is thanks to my surgeon and his great surgical skills. Mel Jennings himself died of a brain tumour that was diagnosed just as he was retiring. How sad that the man who prolonged my life did not have long to enjoy his own.

EIGHTEEN

You expect to be asked if surviving cancer changes you in some fundamental way. Even doctors seem to expect a permanent sunny smile and an obvious zest that wasn't there in the pre-tumour days, when naturally you thought you were immortal. Rather than make big changes, I did decide I was not about to give up the job I adored. It did convince me to say Yes to a lot more invitations. And I don't mean parties – I have never been keen on those – but it does mean that offers of work that I might have rejected once, I now tend to agree to.

There had already been some big events to witness away from the usual news round. Every evening the Belgian fire brigade trumpets Last Post at the Menin Gate in Ypres to remember nearly 55,000 British and Allied troops who perished in the terrible battles around there in World War One. On the 80th anniversary of the end of the war, one poppy for each dead soldier fluttered down from the arch. It was hard to choke back tears. A few old soldiers who had been in the trenches either stood proudly by, or watched from their wheelchairs. Most of them, by now a hundred years old and more, were Canadian. Their survival had to be a testament to the wide open spaces and healthy climate awaiting those who made it back home after the carnage.

Capturing the scene to go with my reporting was a wonderful French cameraman, Fred Nerac. A few years later, he would be killed as the First Iraq War neared its end. Dead alongside him was my ITN colleague Terry Lloyd, and their Lebanese translator. I was on newscasting duty that night. It was the most terrible one in ITN's history.

Lloyd was a fine reporter. Although he did something very different, and passed away in a British hospital rather than amid the chaos of a war zone, the presenter Richard Whiteley was another great loss to television. He died at the age of 61 after heart surgery. His words and numbers quiz show *Countdown* was created to pass a leisurely hour or so in the afternoons and Whiteley had been in the chair from the start. Being a guest on the show has always been a pleasure, although the avuncular Whiteley could be mischievous. Part-way through the show he would chat to the guest. 'What shall we talk about?' he would say as we prepared for the first of five recordings done in a day at the Leeds studio of Yorkshire Television. Whatever you suggested, you could bet he would choose something else, a sly grin on his face as he did so.

Countdown may have become a creaky vehicle for the 21st century. Whiteley would relate how important and usually London-based television executives too busy to watch daytime TV would confess that they didn't know what the programme was all about. 'You will . . . you will,' Whiteley would say, knowing that retired viewers made up a big part of his loyal audience.

If *Countdown* was gentle, *The Weakest Link* was most certainly not. Deliberately so. Anne Robinson is famed for her acid tongue. That's show business. Anne's insults were to be expected. What I had not appreciated was the manner of one's banishment if you did not make it to the end. As you hear the familiar putdown 'You are the weakest link!' you step from a slightly raised stage and walk off into the gloom of a corner of a big studio. Trouble is, you have to do the 'walk of shame' several times as the unseen director orders shots from different cameras to capture the full humiliation of exit.

The second time on *Weakest Link*, scary Anne Robinson actually gave me a kiss after the programme. She is just one of so many people have helped make my 'career' such a marvellous meander. Fleet Street had introduced me to some characters who were less than totally charming; television people, on the other hand, tend to be nice folk, even though competition for the plum spots is intense. Certainly they have been endlessly accommodating to someone who decided to hop over the journalistic divide between the print and the screen. Once my wings started spreading, another clever and charming TV producer enquired if I would like to host my own quiz show. Stephen Leahy made his reputation as a masterly inventor of quiz formats that were major successes. He had worked with Bob Monkhouse on shows like *The Golden Shot*.

He was looking for a host for a series based on television detective shows. There is no shortage of those, and contestants would be tested on their knowledge from Sherlock Holmes to Inspector Morse. We spent a week shooting *Watching the Detectives*. When you work in television news, you get used to money being spent as sparingly as possible. 'Light ent' – light entertainment – tends even these days to splash cash around quite liberally. Chauffeur-driven limousines, and flowers and hampers for TV executives, are expected to be in the budget. Our series was shot in a rambling country house in Cheshire, just the sort of pile where you would expect to find the body in the library. Brenda came along, and a comfortable and highly interesting week we had.

For a newsman, the timing was not ideal. The 7/7 bombings in London happened in the middle of recording. I could not break a contract and desert Leahy's quiz show. Maybe the fates paid me back for not being around for the biggest peacetime news story in the UK, because *Watching the Detectives* struggled in the summertime ratings. A big and tense cricket tournament held most viewers' interest. Nevertheless, insomniacs tell me that repeats of *Detectives* regularly get outings in the small hours of the morning on ITV.

Being part of commercial broadcasting, ITN was always looking for extra sources of income. An early example was when Stewart Purvis, when still boss of Channel Four News, was asked to make a video for, and about, the Treasury. I was chosen to be the reporter. My chief recollection of going into the Chancellor of the Exchequer's domain,

You again? With HM at the London Press Club, 2007. (Picture by London Press Club)

Number 11 Downing Street, was the very cramped downstairs loo I was directed to. Purvis and ITN got into hot water over one bit of filming. We put up the ITN helicopter to inject some glamour into pictures of the Treasury's headquarters in Whitehall. Someone forgot that we were supposed to alert the House of Commons authorities if we were flying over Parliament. The Serjeant at Arms apparently blasted his annoyance in an irate telephone call to some ITN executive.

Another revenue raiser was to offer television-type coverage for big occasions which would not actually find their way on to the ITV network. It was challenging to be the commentator for a Greek Royal wedding. First the producer and I went to meet the exiled Greek King Constantine in his large home close to Hampstead Heath. Exile he may have been, but the house had the atmosphere of a Royal court. We waited in a large sitting room, until a pair of double doors were opened, Constantine was announced, and the monarch without a throne entered.

Having established what he and his family wanted, we set up a vast amount of technical gear in and around the Greek Orthodox cathedral in London's Bayswater. It is an exquisite but small church, so the idea was to relay the ceremony to the many guests who could not fit in. They would view proceedings on big screens at the lavish reception. Most of the Royalty of Europe, including Britain's, made up the congregation that squeezed in to witness the wedding of Crown Prince Pavlos to the daughter of an American billionaire. The service was conducted almost entirely in Greek. My commentary position was underground in St Sophia's musty crypt. An elderly Greek lady sat alongside to help with translation. We both quickly got lost as the order of service we had been given bore scant relation to what was being intoned upstairs. No-one apparently minded. ITN's Greek customers seemed quite happy afterwards. And the music and the singing were superb.

Live commentary is always nerve-wracking. Robert Lacey, the most urbane and knowledgeable of Royal experts, sat alongside me in the cab of an outside broadcast lorry as we commentated together for the wedding in Windsor of Prince Charles and his long-time love, Camilla Parker Bowles. Apart from our cramped accommodation, doing a polished job was almost impossible because we had to rely most of the time on BBC pictures over which ITN had no control. I would begin talking about one shot when the picture would change abruptly to something else. It was complicated by a technical difficulty that meant I could not ask any questions of the ITN control room, even when we in the lorry were not on air. We were broadcasting pretty blind.

Lacey and I reckoned we had done rather well, especially in the trying circumstances. The *Mirror* newspaper thought different. The paper that had published an affectionate near-obituary of me after my operation devoted a whole page to saying what a hesitant and indifferent job we had done. There we go: failing to please all of the people, and so forth. And all this in a newspaper where my stepdaughter Justine was employed as a reporter. The one comfort is an old piece of advice to anyone in the public's sometimes scathing eye. All is fine as long as they spell your name right.

Appearances on a couple of programmes actually terrified me. My wife would observe that my habit of saying Yes is more accurately described as the habit of failing to say No. The most frightening time in front of a camera was when I sat in the big black chair for a round of *Celebrity Mastermind*. Having said my uneasy Yes, I found the process of preparation intriguing. The producer and I negotiated away until we had set the boundaries for a specialist subject that would give me a sporting chance of not looking a complete idiot. There have been occasional mentions of my passion for trains: for *Mastermind* we chose the railways of Southern England. I would love to meet whoever helped compile the questions. Some were fiendish. I did well enough to come a face-saving second to the gardening guru Monty Don. His subject was the Beatles. It was a trifle galling to await my own turn, knowing I could have answered most·of his specialist questions. I bet he would have been stumped if asked which was the first London terminus to open (London Bridge, reached by the London and Greenwich Railway in 1836).

I had broken a golden rule and had a decent lunch with old print colleagues before the afternoon's recording session. I say 'decent' because wine was taken. On just this one occasion I decided alcohol would dull any pain. More alcohol was available after the show. As contestants and production staff milled around the green room, quizmaster John Humphrys sidled up to me. During the recording he had asked me what the initials 'VEP' stood for. I answered promptly. They describe the brakes and carriage formation of a certain type of electric train. 'Vestibule Electro-Pneumatic' won me a point. 'When you knew that,' Humphrys growled, 'I thought: "You sad bastard!"'

Another BBC presenter, Bill Turnbull, used almost the same phrase – he actually said 'You poor bastard' – when I asked for advice about a show he had been in. In 2006, an invitation arrived to appear on BBC Television's biggest entertainment hit. Over tea and scones in Browns Hotel in Mayfair, a persuasive lady producer told me why they wanted me to be on *Strictly Come Dancing*. I was most unsure about it. Lithe sports stars, pretty actresses – these would be my competitors. And they would all be *young*. 'Nick,' she insisted. 'We want you too.' We broke off for a few moments to oblige a giggling hen party who wanted their photographs taken as they guzzled champagne. Then came the determined sell. 'There are two important things to think about,' said the producer. 'One, can you take criticism?' Skin has thickened and shoulders have broadened over the decades spent in the company of sharp-tongued types in newsrooms big and small, national and regional. No problem there. The second thing? 'You get paid the same whether you are out first round, or last to the end.' Further discussion seemed totally unnecessary.

My partner was the highly gifted Nicole Cutler, a petite South African who like all the *Strictly* professionals danced like a dream. I did not, and would not be much better for all her patient tutoring. I had no illusions about surviving beyond the first programme of the new series. There was a vague chance that I might beat an even older competitor, comedian Jimmy Tarbuck. I did stumble around in a less embarrassing excuse for a waltz than he managed. His well-deserved popularity as a very funny man won him the public votes, however. I duly disappeared after round one. Craig Revell Horwood, the judge with the reputation for being the most cutting when a dance is particularly inept, gave me only a couple of points. When we met the next night to go on the BBC2 show which reviewed the goings-on – and goings-off – each week on *Strictly*, I reminded him about his ungenerous scoring. 'Two points?' he said. 'As many as that?'

Mastermind had been hyper-scary, but it was also petrifying to go sweeping out on the dance floor in Television Centre's Studio One, the lessons learned in several weeks of hard rehearsal suddenly dribbling out of my brain. I was sorry Nicole Cutler's great efforts got nowhere. The arduous schedule of preparation for my couple of minutes in front of a huge audience did at least make me fitter than I had ever been before. I ate an awful lot of tuna sandwiches, not my favourite food, to keep my middle-aged energy up.

I think my best performance came just before the actual programme in front of a crowd of local schoolchildren, who came into the gym where

Only briefly: Strictly Come Dancing, with professional partner Nicole Cutler.
(Picture by BBC)

we rehearsed. Their clapping and cheering were so gratifying. So unlike that unappreciative Revell Horwood. No, he was dead right. I was rightly booted. Having admitted that, I would not have missed a moment of my brief encounter with the extraordinary world of the dance. Nor the session in front of inquisitor Humphrys for *Mastermind*. Even so, I cannot hear the introductory music for either of those two shows without getting a dose of the cold shudders.

NINETEEN

There was a moment of great hilarity at the famous lunch with Princess Diana. My ITN editor in chief, Stewart Purvis, motioned towards me and said to her: 'Bet you can't guess what his great interest in life is . . .' She swivelled around to me and her big eyes widened. Purvis added the kicker: 'He loves . . . railways.' Ho, ho, ho all around the table. What had John Humphrys called me? Ah yes: a sad bastard. But here is my challenge. See a steam engine hauling a train, and try not to smile. Everyone does. We are all railway enthusiasts deep down.

After my 'medical adventure' in 2002 I promised myself I would try to spend more time doing things I enjoyed. The wonderful world of radio has been generous to me. I was invited to a host a weekly show on Classic FM, with enthusiastic and knowledgeable young producers to help me. After years of TV, it has been terrific to have people say they like the radio work. To be told you have a good voice for both main types of broadcasting is to me the highest of compliments.

We won't dwell on the frustrations of trying to play better golf: I gave up appearing in most charity matches long ago, soon after an opening shot in front of a big crowd of onlookers struck a tree at full tilt and zoomed back over my head. Going round golf courses with old mates is much more of a pleasure – as long as they promise to look away when I strike a ball. Or try to.

Trains have been much more rewarding. I have adored them in all their diversity. It is not just the more picturesque old railways that fascinate. Modern operations do too, and railways are booming now in a way they have not matched since Victorian times. I have been lucky not only to be invited to inspect the inner workings of many systems but also to meet the people who have helped shape the way we travel when, sensibly, we do it on rails. People like Chris Green, who saw the sense of combining the various lines in London and the South East into a coherent whole for the public to understand, and did so much to make

Inter City the successful flagship of the old British Rail. Privatisation has brought with it some ludicrous insanities, and some breathtakingly high fares. The benefit has been in realising that it is the needs of the passenger that should come first. On many routes that has led to much better services. Some still lag, disgracefully. Green was one who saw the priority of trying to satisfy customers' needs many years ago. Thanks to his friendship I am now an associate member of the Retired Railway Officers' Society, to me a terrific honour.

There has been enormous fun too with those older bits of railway that the British in particular take to their hearts. For a couple of years I laboured away as a fireman on the Bluebell, that treasure of a preserved line in East Sussex. The work of preparing and helping to keep a locomotive going is back-breaking. Once you get going, the swaying footplate is a perilous place. As I struggled to shoot coal into the firebox without losing my balance, a crusty old engine driver once muttered at me: 'Don't fall off. It means paperwork.' I would go home looking as though I had spent a day in a particularly filthy coal mine.

It was early one freezing cold morning, perched some fifteen feet in

Where's my anorak? Memories of footplate duties on the Bluebell Railway.
(Picture by Andy Newbold Photography)

the air cleaning the top of the boiler of an elderly engine, when I realised I had to look for something safer and a little easier. I found it with a Victorian gem. Volk's Railway runs for just over a mile along the sea front in Brighton. It is the oldest electrically-operated line in the world. Like so many, I had lovely memories of riding on it as a child. Its 125th anniversary was in 2008, and I was asked to officiate at the celebrations. I agreed. I had a look round, and became enchanted with this small yet important relic.

Its inventor was a gifted engineer, Magnus Volk, son of a German clockmaker, who can be credited with being the Brunel of electric railway traction. He was a wonderful innovator, even if some of his projects came to grief. After laying out and running some of the line that we see today, he built an incredible contraption nicknamed 'Daddy Long Legs' which was a carriage perched on top of tall steel legs. It ran on widely-spaced rails from the east end of Brighton along the beach towards Rottingdean. The tide would sweep over the track and the whole shebang could only crawl along. Battered by the sea, Daddy Long Legs did not last long. His more straightforward Volk's Railway has survived and it is the greatest thrill for this anorak to be qualified as a driver.

It may be an old-fashioned indulgence. But after many years of amusing people by admitting an enthusiasm for railways I now feel right up to date. Trains are seen as the answer to the transport problems faced by a crowded world which worries about future energy supplies. Mind you, we are talking about trains running a good deal faster than the 13 miles an hour allowed along Brighton sea front.

A golden moment was having Michael Portillo, politician turned media star, visit Volk's for a new series of his railway-based programmes. The artifice of television is part and parcel of my life. So I was good and ready for a filmed encounter with this important man. It was a sparkling summer morning when he turned up on the sea front in a lime green jacket and livid pink shirt. Noticeable, you might say. Portillo and his camera crew approached me as I prepared to drive one of the trains. 'Who have we here?' he enquired as I slid my dark glasses off. 'Ah, it's Nicholas Owen.' After some banter about engine driving being every lad's dream – well, it was once – he ended with a neat phrase: 'Your secret's safe with me.' The camera lingered as I turned back to the controls. 'I fear not,' I said. I knew they would use the whole, irresistible sequence.

Volk's Railway works its charm by staying antiquated. The television business never stands still. In my time, it has been changing constantly.

I have never seen the point of complaining about the way things are done. Whatever you think about individual programmes, production standards – on the big channels anyway – are higher than ever. TV news has to take its place and look slick. And it is a business that has been extraordinarily good to me. Almost every viewer who has bothered to get in touch, or who has met me in the street, has been kind. Even when I get mistaken for someone else, especially for Jon Snow (much taller than me), or Martin Bell (who is never seen out except in a white suit). A barmy opinion poll in *The Sun* a few years back discovered I was Britain's fifth sexiest male newsreader. A cue for hilarity whenever it is mentioned.

Sometimes viewers can have a direct impact on how the news is presented. After the memorial service in York Minster for Richard Whiteley, I came out to be greeted by a group of Yorkshire ladies. They have strong views, usually well put. As I know from my Huddersfield-born wife. Now, there are consulting firms paid large sums to offer advice on the way news programmes should look, and suggest changes. Some things become fashionable. It was decided presenters should not just sit and talk. They should move around the studio. '*Why* do you walk about?' one Yorkshire lady said. The others chimed in, all saying how daft it looked. I thought so too. Back in London I passed on the customers' views. I was not asked to wander around after that.

The most humbling example of a viewer's feelings came thanks to another Yorkshire lady, and one I never met. A letter arrived at ITN from a solicitor, saying that a client had left me all the money in her will. The amount was modest, but the gesture was touching in the extreme. A few enquiries revealed that she had been a widow for years, and television had been an obvious comfort for a lonely soul. For some reason, she liked what I did. I hope her loneliness was not too acute. I think of Betty Hodgson often, and with great fondness.

Her decision came as a big surprise not just to me but also to the Editor of ITV News, David Mannion. He couldn't recall a similar case. Later, I had another surprise for him. When I reached 60, I asked him if I could stay on but work less. After my cancer operation, Mannion – a journalistic genius who had always been so good to me – had declared that I would in future be confined to the studio. No more knackering rounds of reporting. He agreed happily to me continuing to present, if less frequently. Then my old employers, the BBC, suggested a part-time return to the Corporation after a quarter of a century to become a freelance again and front some of their rolling news, with occasional appearances on BBC 1 bulletins and the Breakfast show.

ITN itself had tried to compete with the BBC and with Sky News in the 24-hour news business. As the second war against Iraq ended, I was on air on the ITV News Channel watching ecstatic crowds rampaging through the streets of Baghdad. One man showed his contempt for Saddam Hussein by first slapping a large picture of the hated dictator with his shoe – a time-honoured Arab insult – before thrusting his lower body against Saddam's face. 'I don't think I can refer to what he is doing on national television,' I said to those few viewers who would have been tuned in. Unfortunately, rolling news was a drain on finances that ITV could not accept, and the operation closed at the end of 2005.

Being back at the BBC in the heart of its gigantic news machine has been a splendid way to propel myself towards my half century in a trade which has given me so much. Not many journalists nowadays have been fortunate enough to straddle the worlds of print and broadcasting. To have voyaged from the old Fleet Street to the sharp end of 24-hour TV coverage, to have reported so many domestic and international stories for so many different employers, has been the greatest of great good luck.

The question about meeting the Queen and other Royals has been a recurring one since the mid 1990s. The most unlikely folk are inquisitive. Away from television there has developed a busy freelance business hosting corporate events. These included some years ago chairing discussions aboard a small luxury liner chartered for a trip round the Mediterranean by an American mobile phone company.

Americans are strange to work for. They like to portray themselves as laid back and easy-going. They are not. They are very exacting, and the alarmingly young boss of the mobile firm was very difficult to please. In fact I think he decided early on that I was not to his liking. To entertain their guests his firm hired Lionel Ritchie, no less, to do a special concert on the island of Mallorca. The expense and glamour of such an event was at odds with the difficulties of getting the precious customers and their wives off the ship and into little boats to get to the island itself. The waves were running high, the little boats were lurching up and down. There was a good chance someone would end up in the water. As we finally made it away from the liner, the grumpy Yankee boss turned to me. Told what I did, his eyes widened. He asked the obvious one: 'Hey ... have you actually *met* the Queen?' He suddenly became quite friendly, at least until the next morning and another business session.

The observation I have heard ever since I was scuttling around for my local newspaper is: 'You must meet such interesting people.' It still comes up almost every time with the lovely and gratifyingly interested audiences who come along to my one-man theatre show. Incidentally, if you buy a ticket, stand by for the piano playing. My answer to the queries about interesting encounters has to be: absolutely, yes. And some of the most interesting have been among most people's least favourite individuals. Perhaps at the bottom of public regard would be murderers. I once spent a day at a prison in Rutland, giving a talk to life prisoners about current affairs. Very well-informed they were too, having had plenty of time to watch the news, I suppose. And most were open about the crime that had got them locked away. Only one quite elderly man said nothing at all, and stared into space away from me when I was talking. It was explained he had never repented of the murder he had committed, and would therefore never be released.

Although not quite so low in the opinion polls, journalists as a species are way down in the public's esteem, not helped at all by the News International scandals of 2011. However, it is interesting that television newsreaders score almost higher than anyone else. A bit confusing. Much clearer is what the opinion polls say about MPs. They were low in popular regard even before the expenses scandals of 2009 and 2010. The *Daily Telegraph* got scoop after scoop unearthing what so many parliamentarians were up to. I have always been happy with the view that the relationship between journalism and politics should be that of a dog to a lamp post. That is not to say I hold all politicians in contempt. Far from it. Most at least start out convinced that they have the chance to do some good, to come up with new ideas that will make life better. Few manage to do much. The complexities of modern existence – especially the media's relentless spotlight – make political decision-making ever more fraught. So while I have meandered around looking for lamp posts, I have admired the tenacity and commitment of the majority of the politicians I have met.

The process started early. Harold Macmillan was prime minister from the late 1950s into the 1960s, and an early journalistic urge had me seek him out at a garden fete he was opening in his constituency of Bromley in Kent. Ban the Bomb supporters chanted away as 'Supermac' arrived. CND demonstrators were not seen as any real threat, and the few detectives guarding the Conservative leader were quite relaxed as a young schoolboy loomed up, waited his moment, and took a picture with a

My first PM: my own 'snap' of Harold Macmillan.

brownie box camera. The moustachioed, wily old PM was caught pretty well. He and I shared a birthday – February 10th – which gave me a great opportunity. I sent the 'snap' of him to his home at Birch Grove, mentioned the birthday connection, and back came a treasured signature.

So I can claim to have met every Prime Minister since Macmillan – and interviewed every one since Harold Wilson. Wilson himself had a sad decline. It was realised years later that his unexpected retirement was due to the onset of senility. I had a small hint of it. After he had left Downing Street, we met at some City function. It was in that madcap period when I was working for James Goldsmith and *Now!* magazine. I hoped the former PM had noticed the magazine. What did he think of it? He stopped, and considered the question. 'How much is it?' he asked eventually. It did not seem the most important point when considering Goldsmith's ambitions to be a new force in the British media.

One of Wilson's closest Cabinet allies was Denis Healey, sometime Labour Defence Secretary, and a notable Chancellor of the Exchequer during a period of extreme economic difficulty. His studio speciality was when the camera was trained on the interviewer rather than himself, he would pull faces, and even stick his tongue out. If the piece was being recorded, some shots were done for editing purposes, without sound being recorded. On several occasions, as I tried to look serious as if listening to the Great Man discourse on the political arguments of the day, he would begin a ribald joke. I always managed not to corpse.

The most memorable encounters had to be with Margaret Thatcher. I was a guest at a Downing Street reception in her Prime Ministerial days, and realised why that toughest of ladies could dominate a male Cabinet. She had sex appeal, helped by her being shorter than you might have expected. A man a little taller than a woman usually feels protective towards her. Or we used to: today's men would probably be forced to deny any such idea.

It was when she had left office that I had my most interesting meeting with the by-then Baroness Thatcher. She set up an office a mile or two away from the Houses of Parliament, in a smart, large house in Belgravia. Going to interview here there, she might as well have been in her full pomp in Downing Street. Police officers roamed the street outside, charming young men greeted the visitor, other flunkeys showed you to her office. As I climbed up a wide staircase, I spotted her husband Denis in the hallway below. The scene was a classic. He was whirling an umbrella in imitation of a golf swing. Everyone knew that was his life-long pastime. 'How is it? How's the swing?' I asked. He looked up, pulled a face, and said that arthritis was ruining his game. Poor him. My own golf has always been ruined by sheer incompetence.

Once inside Margaret Thatcher's very large office I was struck by the overriding theme of almost every picture, ornament and gift on display. It was the Falklands War, and its victorious outcome. Recapturing the Falklands helped Mrs Thatcher to win the 1983 General Election. She beat a Labour party led by a stalwart of the movement, Michael Foot.

When he died in March 2010 I remembered going with a BBC crew to film him giving an election speech in Cumbria. Foot had many virtues. A gift of oratory was one of them, but it is a gift not well suited to the sound bite age. As is customary, a copy of his speech was given to me by one of his staff. I scanned through, knowing that the main BBC bulletins would be looking for 15 or so good, clear seconds. I spotted a perfect passage. Knowing Foot's propensity to skate off into soaring ad libs, I sidled up and asked if he would please stick to that bit of script, if he wanted to be on the *Nine O'Clock News*. Yes, he said, no problem. Once he stood up, and a loyal crowd cheered and clapped, his assurance was forgotten. His old-fashioned way of lurching away from a prepared text made for a fine speech, but a perfect nightmare for a TV reporter trying to find a sensible clip for transmission.

Michael Foot was saddled with a deeply divided party and a manifesto described by the Labour MP Gerald Kaufman as 'the longest suicide note in history'. It was certainly out of tune with an electorate which had definitely turned Right, making Foot relatively easy for Margaret Thatcher to beat. A much harder tussle had been the one she had against the man she supplanted as Tory leader. It was the climax of that contest that I had witnessed in the lobby of the Commons back in the mid 1970s. Ted Heath found it impossible to conceal his resentment for the rest of his days. He lived eventually in a spectacularly lovely house in the cathedral close in Salisbury. ITN wanted him interviewed about Thatcher, and after the usual rigmarole with armed policemen at his gate, the crew and I were shown into a sunlit sitting room, dominated by a grand piano. Music had been one of Heath's two great passions outside politics. The fact that he did have outside interests made him unusual in a line of work that tends to attract obsessive personalities.

Heath's other love was sailing, which saved the day, and the interview. His habitual grumpiness had been greatly sharpened by painful trouble with one of his legs. He clumped around slowly and in a very disagreeable mood. His temper would hardly be improved by having to talk about his old nemesis. Before the camera started running, I looked over the many pictures crowding the top of his piano. In pride of place was one of *Morning Cloud*, the yacht in which he had often raced. 'Sailor Ted', as this formidable man was sometimes called, became animated, almost friendly, as we talked of his experiences under sail. The interview went ahead smoothly.

Heath would not be drawn into any recriminations against his successor. It was different when the camera was turned off. 'When you heard Margaret Thatcher had resigned,' I said to him, 'I was told you did say to your staff: "Rejoice". Was that right?' There was an awkward silence. Sailor Ted's brow clouded. The cameraman stopped packing up his gear, and sucked in a nervous breath. Eventually the priceless answer came back. Not one he would have made if that camera had still been turned on. 'No. What I said to them was ... "Rejoice, rejoice, *rejoice!*"'

Long after Heath, Thatcher herself was elbowed out in favour of John Major. His rival in the 1992 election was Neil Kinnock, who was sure, along with the rest of the Labour party, that he could see off this dithering Tory, so unlike the Iron Lady, Thatcher. On election night I was at the constituency count that finished early and signalled beyond doubt that Labour would be the losers. It was at Basildon in Essex. My daughter Rebecca, then aged 22, came along with a friend. It was a good opportunity to witness democracy in action. As the Conservative supporters cheered triumphantly at the decisive win for their candidate David Amess, it was obvious Major's Tories would stay in power.

The next day, I toured the constituency with the Oxford academic Professor Vernon Bogdanor. For him it was a rare, and enjoyable, chance to study the realities of politics on the ground rather than in theory. Almost every voter we approached was clear why they had voted Tory. Major may not have wowed anyone. But they thought Labour's Neil Kinnock would be a disaster. It was the same gut feeling of dislike that put paid to Gordon Brown's premiership in 2010.

John Major was a strange mixture of a Prime Minister. Although he had a reputation around Westminster for ruthlessness, there was a nervousness rare among those who kick and stab their way to the top of the greasiest of poles. Much later there would be universal surprise about his clandestine affair with fellow Tory Edwina Currie. He just did not seem the type somehow. Among Major's public crises was the worst Royal one since the abdication of Edward VIII. As ITN's Royal Correspondent I went to talk to Major in Number Ten just after he had announced formally to MPs that the Prince and Princess of Wales were getting divorced. The questions were straightforward, his answers unsurprising but apposite. Great sadness that the Royal marriage had come to this, time for both parties to move on, seek future happiness, and so forth. When the camera was turned off, I thanked the Prime Minister, and stood up. He remained in his chair, looking worried. 'Was that really all right?' he said. 'Do you think we should do it again?' Not what you expect from someone wrestling with awesome decisions hour by hour at the heart of Government.

Major, as he put himself, left the stage when the curtain came down for him and the Conservatives in 1997. The Tony Blair years, to bring so much hope and eventually so much rancour, began. He started his climb up the political ladder by enjoying one of the few triumphs amid the wreckage of so many Labour hopes in the 1983 Election. He became the new MP for Sedgefield in the North East. An early appointment for the ambitious young member of the Commons was in the Newcastle studio of the BBC. He spoke to me about the need to abolish capital punishment in schools. *Corporal* punishment, he meant of course. He managed to smile graciously as I corrected the future Labour leader as politely as I could, live on air.

When Blair had been in Downing Street for several years, we had an encounter which was alarming for him and nerve-wracking for me. He was to declare open a new Virgin rail service. Tilting trains would be bringing down journey times substantially, after the spending of vast sums – way over budget – on modernising the West Coast Main Line. The ceremony was at Euston station, starring that master of publicity, Richard Branson. Someone among his staff came up with a special wheeze. Would I be prepared to do a mini version of *This Is Your Life* for another participant, Branson's Virgin rail chief, Chris Green? I agreed, happy to honour the friend who has been the best and brightest railwayman of my generation. The idea was to stand up mid-way through the proceedings, and pay a surprise tribute to the unsuspecting Green.

I spotted straightaway a great possible complication. I told Virgin staff they had to warn Blair, and his police guard, what would happen. Otherwise, I ran a real risk of being wrestled to the ground like that deranged protestor in front of Prince Charles in Sydney. And a flying

Worrying a PM: a surprise speech, with Sir Richard Branson and Tony Blair.
(Picture by Virgin Rail)

tackle was the better option. A worse one was that I could be shot. I was assured Blair and his entourage would all be fully briefed. He was very closely guarded, everyone mindful that Blair's popularity was waning sharply after the miscalculations over the second Iraq war.

As I rose from my place in the front row of the audience, I saw a brief look of horror in the eyes of the Prime Minister. No-one had tipped him off after all. He must have wondered for a few brief seconds if, whoever else he feared, his assassin was going to be that friendly Nicholas Owen. Thrillers often feature killers groomed for many years as 'sleepers', before they carry out a dastardly act. Afterwards, introducing him to my wife, I apologised if he had been startled. 'No problem,' Blair said. 'Always the true professional, you.'

The rough and tumble of politics left Tony Blair roaming the Middle East as a peace negotiator when he was not earning fat fees at various speaking engagements. Trying to get much out of the new PM while he had been Chancellor of the Exchequer had always been fairly fruitless. Gordon Brown had contributed to my well-being in a way that had nothing to do with the economy. One evening when I had finished my work at ITN headquarters I had to change into a dinner suit to go to some function. I have a lifelong dislike of such outfits, not helped by always having a struggle getting a bow tie done up. Checking the time, I realised Channel Four News was on the air, meaning the programme's make-up lady would be at her post and could help. When I went into the Channel Four green room, make-up was absent: presumably she was in the studio making sure Jon Snow was looking his usual sleek self. To my rescue came the next guest waiting be grilled by Snow. A sympathetic Chancellor and Prime Minister-in-waiting did a quick and very compet-ent job of sorting out my tie. Impressive for a man notorious for refusing to don formal clobber for big City occasions. And Gordon Brown's detractors should note it was all done with the broadest of smiles.

Sometimes the world of politics and the media become wrapped up together. My first producer when I arrived at Channel Four News was Damian Green. He did not stay very long, heading off to work for the Tories, eventually becoming a minister after the Coalition victory in the 2010 election. A friend who is a senior civil servant in the Home Office mentioned to Green those television days with me when they sat together at a Government conference. 'Ah yes,' he said. 'They were good times.'

TWENTY

Giving advice to those who think they want to be journalists has become extremely tricky. There has never been more media, and therefore more opportunities. But money is short, and getting shorter everywhere. As other forms of communication rise, as the internet sweeps all before it, the decline of newspapers has been painful to watch. When I quit ITN I was bowled over by a leaving gift from two old mates from 'the print'. Arthur Edwardes, *The Sun*'s celebrated Royal photographer, and reporter Charles Rae presented me with a fake front page. It has all the bold hallmarks of a classic issue of *The Sun*. The big headline is 'Owen Up', the copy underneath is suitably rude, and a trailer at the top invites readers to 'follow Nick's dodgy journey through life: pages 2, 3, 4 and 5.'

The picture captured a bizarre moment in the ITN studio. I was presenting alongside the delightful Katie Derham. It was Lunchtime News, so we sometimes covered stories that were, shall we say, lighter. One lunchtime, a mother came in with her very small child to discuss some problem or other confronting parents. After the interview was over, the child decided to hop out of her arms and dash around the studio. The unflappable Katie scooped the small one up. And we read some closing headlines, both there in vision, me half-grinning, Derham looking cheerful and businesslike with our young studio guest on her lap.

The mocked-up front page was the ultimate present for an old hack. My daughter Rebecca could have made a journalist, I know. She was not keen on the disruption to family life she had witnessed. She married a fire officer and has done a beltingly good job as a wife and mother. My son Anthony is a policeman in London, also very happily wed. Brenda's son Daniel is a successful businessman. One of our four children, Brenda's daughter Justine, followed her mother and stepfather and spent several years writing for the *Daily Mirror*. I admire her for being a better and tougher reporter than I ever was.

An ideal gift: the mocked-up front page on leaving ITN, 2007.

Coming up fast on the outside lane are the grandchildren. For the woman I have called for more than 50 years my mother – my stepmother Diana – that brings her the joy of being a great grandparent. How I wish my father had lived many more years, to see me settled again after my divorce, to see a wonderfully happy new marriage, and to see the newest generation flourishing. Writing a memoir is bound to put powerful

Coming up fast: the grandchildren, 2011.

Now we go to film premieres: with Brenda, London, 2009.

kindling under long-buried memories. I think of my Dad every day. And of my poor mother Edna, dead so long ago. Only recently I have discovered where she died. In the 1950s, North Downs Hospital in Caterham, only a few miles from where I live today, had cared for the chronically sick. The records of who was a patient have long disappeared. But I do now know that Edna was among them, ending her life somewhere among the airy, high-ceilinged rooms of what must once have been a very grand private house.

Struggling to remember the past in more detail seems an inevitable part of growing old oneself. As a dutiful son of 63, I suggested to Diana that she might need more of my help to deal with day to day irritations. 'Thank you Nicholas,' she said. 'But I know you are always so busy. And *you* are not getting any younger . . .' When your Mum says that, it must be time to take notice.

For those grandchildren, it is hard – no, impossible – to foresee how they will be getting their news in the years ahead. The giddy world of the expanding internet and mobile telephony is changing the game fast. Some things have a longer history than you might imagine. Way back in the 1990s, when I was ITN Royal Correspondent, a technically-minded senior colleague, Garron Baines, suggested I write pieces for the-then new ITN website. He knew that the couple of minutes of the average TV item meant that a lot you learn gets left out. Here was the chance to tell more. Maybe I can claim to have been the first proper blogger. We invited viewers to join me online, to ask me questions. I don't think we had a name for that process. Later they were called web chats.

Amid the avalanche of information and misinformation on the 21st century World Wide Web, I reckon presenters of some sort will still be needed. What I am sure of is that older colleagues, mostly retired ones, get it wrong if they think modern newscasting is an overrated, overpaid occupation. Once it was only necessary to read an autocue with a degree of panache and deal with the occasional technical upset. So much more is demanded today. Live interviews come thick and fast for those who ride the rolling news roundabout. Keeping your head when a big story comes in takes steady nerves and extreme concentration. Good journalism has never been more vital. You need the 'well stocked mind' emphasised by my old ITN chief David Nicholas.

And you must try not to say the wrong thing. I was in the News 24 studio – renamed later the BBC News Channel, a brand slow to catch on – when we were advised that we would be getting some live pictures of an important meeting in The Ukraine. Rolling news channels are addicted to any live events they can broadcast – sometimes too much so, I have to say – and I had to do some rapid hunting through the memory. Russia and the Ukraine? Always a tetchy relationship. For decades Ukraine had been a mostly unhappy partner in the old Soviet empire. Now independent again, the struggling country was having a lot of bother with big brothers in Moscow over gas supplies and prices. There had been some kissing and making up, and Russia's dour President Putin had gone to Kiev to be nice to the Ukrainians.

The pictures began running. The unsmiling Putin was striding alongside the woman who was then the Ukrainian Prime Minister, Yulia Tymoshenko. He was quite short. She towered over him. A striking, statuesque blonde, with her hair done up in a hoop, she looked positively Nordic. Scratching for something to say as they paced along an endless corridor in some gaudy palace, I remarked on the contrast between them. The word I used about Ms Tymoshenko after groping for an appropriate one was 'fetching'. A BBC high-up later pulled me to one side. My remark about the imposing female PM was not acceptable. 'You are allowed to think it,' he said. 'You mustn't say it.'

I did a lot better with another Russian drama. 'Boris Yeltsin has died. Go!' The whisper had come from our staff in Moscow. There was nothing from the news agencies, whose reports pour forth every minute of the day and night on the computer screens on the presenters' desk. The BBC were confident it was true. We would be breaking the news, an expression much overused amid the clamour of so many sources of information. This time it was valid. We had a scoop. We would only have it for a few minutes, until our fast-moving rivals spotted what we were saying and followed suit. It was far too early for any script. My job was to fire up the brain cells and talk about the Boris we had known.

Four basic facts whirled around my mind. Yeltsin had been a senior Communist apparatchik who fell out with and triumphed over Mikhail Gorbachev; he was the first democratically-elected president of Russia after the Soviet Union had broken up; he stood on a tank to rally support to thwart a counter coup in Moscow; and he was over-fond of vodka. Many of his countrymen and women were ashamed of his drinking habits and his tendency to clown around.

As BBC backroom staff struggled to find picture material and started rushing correspondents into studios from Moscow to Washington, I had to keep talking. It was Boris Yeltsin, drunkard, that was the characteristic of the man which came to mind more than anything else. There was one tiny worm of doubt. As I continued my off-the-cuff tour of Boris Yeltsin's see-saw career, as colleagues dashed about to get this big story done properly, I wondered vaguely whether I had the correct rotund and powerfully-built Russian. Yeltsin ... now he wasn't the bloke with the red splash on his balding head was he? No, that was Gorbachev, surely. No-one yelled a correction into my earpiece, so I ploughed on.

Finally, help arrived. From the control room the director announced: 'We have the Hanrahan obit. Go to it!' This was a carefully-crafted piece compiled by one of the BBC's finest, the late and exceptionally talented Brian Hanrahan, famous for counting out and counting back British planes during the Falklands War. His work would be well done, and very important, it would buy us all a few minutes' thinking time. A pause, a glance down at scripts which actually had nothing to do with a Russian president, red mark or not, and I introduced the obituary. 'Brian Hanrahan now looks back at his life ...' Relief. Only for a few seconds, though. Hanrahan's report froze. Not a grand time for a technical glitch. Back to the presenter. 'Sorry about that. We will return to Brian Hanrahan's piece in a moment. Meanwhile, if you have just joined us, let me tell you we are hearing that Boris Yeltsin ...' And so on.

There is a grainy old sequence from one of the big American networks of a news 'anchor' – the word saying everything about the elevated status of presenters in the US – having an uncomfortably difficult time. He opens, suitably gravely, with a story about political fisticuffs in Washington. A correspondent will tell us more. Except he doesn't. The line to the White House correspondent disappears. The anchor man apologises, promises to return to the important subject, and launches into another tale about some natural disaster elsewhere in America. Another reporter fails to show. The presenter's eyes betray the first hints of anxiety as he introduces a major story abroad. Yet again, pictures and sound from the third reporter are for some reason unavailable.

The anchor looks slowly back into his camera. And he declares: 'Mother said there would be days like this.'

Brilliant. I hope I am still working long enough in some studio somewhere to use it myself.

INDEX